abby kamen

generation
WE

healing together
to create better

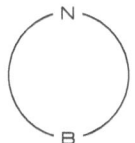

Published with Numinous Books.

Cover design art provided by Ancizar Marin

Interior layout by Chriswilliamsdesign.co.uk

ISBN: 979-8-9868302-3-0

www.numinous-books.com

for the future

contents

introducing generation WE

I am who I have always been, but I have not always been me.

Can anyone else relate?

I awoke one day and found myself staring at a stranger in the mirror. Over time I came to realize the image looking back at me was unrecognizable because it was stamped with a series of labels that prevented my soul from being seen. Not because of the labels themselves per se, but because of the limitations they placed on me appreciating and expressing the full spectrum of my being.

My gender, my skin, my religion, my orientation, my size, my abilities, my health, my wealth, and my age. Each of these labels came to represent a bar on the cage to my soul. Some offered me privilege, acceptance, and safety. Others offered me persecution, rejection, and danger. *Why*? It was a question I could no longer ignore.

What I've come to understand is that the pages of our collective history have sharp edges. Whether it's due to papercuts or severed limbs, we are each carrying the pain of our ancestors and the cyclical nature of survivalism. The problem is generational, but it has nothing to do with the concept of the generations.

In fact, identifying as part of any one generation—Boomer, X, Millennial, Z—merely speaks to a set of cultural reference points that define how we, humans, have reacted to certain sets of internal and external stimuli. Historical events, like wars; natural disasters, like droughts; social mores, like segregation; economics, like inflation; technology, like cell phones; etc. all come to define the values and behaviors of our lived reality.

On the surface it can appear as if each new generation is literally living in a different world and speaking a different language. But are we, really? *We* are still and have always been *us*: all part of the same species. I want to belong, to feel safe, to feel respected, to embrace connection, and to experience love. You too, right?

The notion that my age, or the age I was born in, makes me either wise or out of touch simply is not true. My physical body, and the circumstances of my life, are merely the container of my evolution—yours too.

The presumed generation gap is not what keeps us trapped in a perpetual game of tug-of-war between progress and reversion; it is the generational trauma we continue to pay forward. The rope pulling us apart is the fear that we don't belong, and it is strangling us. This fear is a by-product of what we have come to call civilization, and the systems of hierarchies that have governed our human experience since the beginning of time.

These systems have us mired in the illusion of what it means to be the *perfect* human—the human that belongs, the human that is worthy of receiving protection, nourishment, and pleasure. As a result, we continue to teach bigotry, misogyny, homophobia, xenophobia, and all the other crap that keeps us besting one another in our efforts to feel worthy.

Generation after generation we face the same traumas, because we have yet to heal them. Generation after generation we feel not enough, because we have yet to understand our inherent worth in all of its complexities.

It doesn't matter how old you are, what gender you identify as, the color of your skin, who you love, how you pray, or where you live. We are each affected by a history that has schooled our brains to act and react in a binary manner: that is, to believe there are only two options available at any given moment in time, one which is good, the right way, and one that is bad, the wrong way. This thought pattern has us stuck in absolutes that don't support or reflect the true nature of our beings.

As a result, our trauma keeps playing out louder and louder within us, in the form of anxiety, and around us, in the vitriol of the world stage.

From the pandemic, to police brutality, to record numbers of mass shootings, and all the other forms of destruction currently bombarding us, it can feel like humanity is done for. But, I contend the opposite. Instead of the end of times being upon us, I think we are witnessing the beginning of a new era—an age that recognizes and welcomes us living as our authentic selves.

I believe our potential to shift into a more comprehensive

understanding of our humanness has never been greater. The time to engage our emotional intelligence and sixth sense is now, and we are equipped to make the transition. This may sound daunting, but I know I am experiencing a shift in my consciousness and I can see that many others are too.

Humanity is at a precipice. We have outgrown the camps of elders vs. youths, and all the other divides among us. To survive going forward, we will need to thrive, which entails existing as our full spectrum selves.

Thrival requires us to address the entirety of our needs. Yes, food, shelter, clothing, and belonging are critical, but those barely cover the basics. To embrace our higher needs, such as self-actualization, healing, and transcendence of binary limitations, we must satisfy our needs for respect, creativity, and wonder as well.

Where we are headed is more of a come-as-you-are party. And while everyone is invited, attendance is both optional and voluntary.

I believe the vast terrain of our mental health and well-being is the next frontier for our growth as a species. Conscious evolution is the manifestation of our emotional fitness. I hope you will join me in my desire to become in better shape: body, mind, and soul. The work is intergenerational, intersectional, and intentional. Come prepared to stretch every fiber of your being as you learn and unlearn, as you feel and heal.

My vision for Generation WE is this: we stop being shitty to ourselves and each other and instead we focus on being authentically us. The stories and observations in these pages are designed to bear witness to what generational trauma looks like, and provide insight into ways we can change our behavior to create a more humane world. As always, the way *forward* is through.

We can create better, but WE will have to create it together.

1
crisis

I can pinpoint the inception of my existential crisis to a specific date and time. An astrologer could have a field day with the serendipity. It was March 18, 2015, around 1pm. As it happened, fifty-four years, one day, and one hour from the exact moment I entered the world, ass backwards. Yes, I was a breech babe, which seems very on brand. Although I would spend most of my life trying valiantly to conform, I experienced the world through an alternative lens from the get-go.

My birthday in and of itself is loaded with uniquely significant meaning to me. March 17th, St. Patrick's Day. A day devoted to the rainbow and infused with promises of joy, fortune, luck, and magic. It was also, coincidentally (or not), my grandfather's favorite day of the year. I am named after him and was born a year after his untimely death from a heart attack at age forty-nine.

He owned a curtain and drapery shop with my grandmother. As my mother aged into the business, she assumed the role of his partner. His death was devastating for her and her family; she gave herself twenty-four hours to grieve. Within forty-eight hours she had the business under control, along with a game plan for how it would support her, my biological father, my grandmother, and my uncle who was in his freshman year at college. She was twenty-three.

Anyway, the day before my existential crisis hit, my son Chad and I went before the Kentucky DMV to lobby for a specialty license plate that would provide financial resources and awareness for hunger relief. We live in Louisville, and at the time there was no government funded programming in place, which was absurd given that our state had one of the highest poverty rates in the country.

My involvement in this cause had begun with Chad and his ten-year-old interest in food. *Top Chef* was our favorite show and we would head to Whole Foods to purchase the ingredients and duplicate the recipes. When asked what resonated with him for a bar mitzvah project, the answer came to him quickly.

Chad was concerned that food was being overlooked as the fundamental cornerstone to our well-being. Meals together were being obliterated, eating disorders were running rampant, and so many, despite an abundance of food waste, were going hungry. The situation was both devastating and ridiculous.

I shared his concern and was able to guide his enthusiasm into a project we called "Team Food Chain." "Team" was the operative word; Chad and I instinctively knew how to "work" together. He was eleven and I was forty-eight. We also recognized that the hunger relief landscape didn't need another organization doing programming. What was needed was a unit, a dedicated team, to pull organizations together to share resources and avoid duplicating efforts.

So that's what we did, and our impact was notable. We helped push legislation, connected grassroots and mainstream organizations, reminded folks to eat together whenever possible, raised a good amount of funding, and increased awareness about food insecurity. Our personalities complimented each other beautifully. I brought passion and marketing nous. Chad brought charisma and facts. We alternated between analytics, intuition, vision, and drive. I could work a deal and Chad could speak to a crowd.

Oh, our "mother and son" team had great curb appeal. On paper we checked all the boxes—me the wind beneath his all-American, "president someday" vibe. Because of who we were to each other, and in spite of it, the world opened up to us and we were able to make shit happen.

Until it exploded in our faces. On my birthday. The License Plate for Hunger Relief was rejected, after it had been hushed as a shoo-in. This moment had been years in the making, and it was the second time we had come before the DMV. It was rejected the first time because we'd tried to get it approved through the public sector. We were told that was unacceptable, because a plate for hunger relief didn't warrant such an initiative from the government. Hunger was a private sector issue.

Food insecurity isn't the responsibility of the state?! Okay, no problem, we are citizens, we got this. And so, we formed a 501(c)3, set about raising 25,000 dollars, and getting 900 folks to sign a petition and agree that, if provided, they would purchase the plate, because they felt Kentucky needed organized and ongoing hunger relief funding.

It was an enormous undertaking. Chad even wrote a song entitled "Lionheart" which got the attention of Teddy Abrams, the director of the Louisville orchestra. It was hoped they'd collaborate and use the song to promote the plate initiative. Additionally, we were a few degrees of separation from our hometown pride, actress Jennifer Lawrence. Could we engage her to do a PSA? Hopes were high.

Chad, now almost seventeen, looked handsome and confident as we entered the room at the DMV. He was clutching a notebook that contained the signatures, the money, and a copy of his song lyrics, which we had used for promo material. We were up last and they'd misspelled his name. It wasn't a good omen. Still, he remained optimistic and self-assured.

He stood proud as he presented his materials. The room congratulated him on his accomplishments. And then the chairperson delivered the news. It was a NO. Our fundraising efforts were questioned, even though we'd been told we could combine personal and corporate support. Even though every other specialty plate was funded the same way.

It was also implied that Chad and I were doing this to get him into a good college. Chad choked up at their insinuation and sat down next to me. He couldn't respond. It took all of his effort not to run from the room. Years of hard labor down the tubes, and his integrity challenged.

He was ashen. I took over. I threw the lyrics to his song on the table and questioned *their* integrity. They were abashed, thanked me too for my efforts, but still, they did not believe our case warranted a plate. They liked the design, but didn't trust our mother/son team to get a sustainable number of plates purchased. We were told to try again when we could show we had more "skin in the game."

Seriously? There were other political reasons behind their "no," and neither Chad nor I had any intention of going any further with the project.

***

The hour-long ride home felt like an eternity. Tears rolled down my face as I kept looking over at him, as if to make sure he was still in the car. We made our calls to school, to my husband Craig, to Chad's sister Samantha, and to my mom Roberta; Team Food Chain was a family and a community affair. Everyone was devastated. We calmed them down and bravely reasoned that it wasn't meant to be. We still had the funds, we had done good work, we needed a minute to figure out next steps.

It was also still my birthday, and we went to dinner trying to shake off the astonishing rejection. We tried to laugh. We tried to make jokes about the absurdity of governments, the corruption surrounding them, and this misuse of power— the same political BS that keeps society moving forward at a snail's pace.

Chad took the following day, March 18th, off from school for us to regroup. He rejected an offer from a local democratic representative who'd supported our case to play things out in the media. He informed me that he would not be used as a political football. "I can't let my ego get in the way of my vision," he stated.

It wasn't that his ego wasn't relevant; his sense of self was terribly important to his purpose. It was also deeply wounded by the rejection. But he intuitively knew that if he let his wounded ego get in the way of his desire to help people, what we had achieved would be overshadowed.

Instead, we made plans to give the 25,000 dollars we'd raised for the DMV directly to the organizations that would have benefited from the plate initiative. While we wouldn't be able to offer them sustainable funding going forward, we could offer an immediate boost. A win nonetheless.

The whole chapter did garner Chad a number of accolades, too. He had already won some national and local philanthropic awards and more followed. His *lionhearted* belief in community and change was well received. His very bright future remained secure.

Me? I WAS LOST.

Team Food Chain helped me feel like I had finally arrived, after taking twenty years out of the workforce to have a family. I am well aware that this was my free-will choice. As a humanitarian, I have always been motivated to understand what it meant to be human and my place in it all. Having kids gave me this. As an artist, I loved not having a "job" and the freedom and time to create in a myriad of diverse ways. But as a member of society, I'd felt dismissed as a full-time mom. My job was meeting the needs of others. I didn't realize I was drowning by not adequately meeting my own needs. I thought all I needed was a *real* job and a business card to give me the street cred I felt I was lacking. I had banked my future identity on Team Food Chain. Without it, I didn't know what would become of me.

An answer of sorts arrived when the universe called in my number.

Driving home from lunch that day, we were stopped at a red light. The car in front of us had the license plate "5O1C3." What?! Chad grabbed a photo to prove that we weren't seeing things. It seemed like a highly unusual coincidence. Maybe I wasn't so lost. Maybe this was a sign. Maybe the 501(c)3 we had created wasn't for naught. Maybe this was all taking us somewhere, taking me somewhere.

Well, it was the beginning of what I can only describe as a spiritual storm. From that point on, a steady flow of *signs* in the form of random incidents and coincidences confronted me daily, each delivering a unique message that seemed designed exclusively for me.

More license plates appeared, so many that I started to keep a file: "Realm, Bless, Enjoy, Why, Listen." When I looked at the clock, it frequently read 11:11 and 4:44, number sequences that I learned were thought to be delivering mystical guidance. My horoscope, which I had never read that often, would find its way to me and offer advice like "just believe" and "you're here to do something important."

Folks also began telling me I was "very open." They would find me in line at the grocery, be serving me at a restaurant, or plop down next to me on an airplane. Songs that turned out to have great significance would get stuck in my head. I would be awakened in the middle of the night with an intense desire to investigate topics like sacred geometry, for which I had no point of reference. One night, I must have forgotten to turn off the TV; I awoke abruptly to a clip from a movie instructing me to "follow my destiny."

Follow my destiny ...

What the fuck did that *really* mean? Specifically though, for me? As the weeks went by, I found myself being haunted by the Big Four existential questions that have plagued humanity forever: *Who am I? Why am I here? Where am I going? Why should I give a shit?*

I was despondent. I was having a really difficult time giving a shit, because I felt like shit. At the center of this was the fact that I felt I was not enough. I began to realize that up until the DMV calamity, I had been operating on cruise control. My job and my purpose had been "mom, daughter, sister, wife, friend, volunteer." These labels were my career, my story, my life. My art, my creativity, my passion, my heart, and my brain—I had used them plenty. But, because my efforts came in the package of *housewife*, my work felt insignificant.

That said, my ego was starving and I needed a purpose, I needed to belong. Frankly, I also needed a job. How was I going to fill my days? Folks confused my angst with a longing for my kids to be young again, a symptom of the fabled "empty nest." Are you kidding me? I didn't want to be "needed" anymore, by anyone. I wanted to be. I wanted to be ME and I didn't know who that was.

But if I'd felt abandoned by the universe that day in the DMV, now it was responding by leaving clues as to what the answers to my existential inquiry might be. The license plates, both the one that didn't happen and the weirdly "coincidental" one we saw, came to represent the moment of my "awakening." Apparently, I was ready to meet me: the me of my highest self.

***

I know this kind of language can sound very woo, but I found it comforting. It helped to explain the bizarre series of events that had begun to infiltrate my life. I was a babbling brook of serendipities; I could communicate with the beyond! But I quickly learned not everyone found my awakening to my energetic gifts as fascinating as I did. Not even those who presented themselves as being in the business of the beyond.

Like the time in 2019 when I attended SXSW. I showed up to the week-long conference in various ensembles of trendy white. I was going for the modern-day *earth angel* look. Cringe. It was also easy to mistake me as part of the cast from *Good Omens*, who were walking the streets to promote their new TV show.

Anyway, I was certain my moment to shine would be at a session titled "Write The Future Now." Featuring a distinguished panel of sci-fi film makers and futurists, the session was centered around deep philosophical inquiry regarding our human plight, AI, our relationship to the beyond, and the possibility of contact with other intelligent lifeforms.

This was my new wheelhouse! My energy was hectic. I popped in and out of my seat, alternately agreeing and disagreeing with their visions of the future. Could I convince them to write a narrative that didn't scare the shit out of people? Why was everything a dystopia? If they really could "write the future," why weren't they creating positive scenarios? Why weren't they enlightening folks about the benefits of energy healing, intuitive wisdom, and extrasensory perception?

When the moderator offhandedly stated, "Mother Nature

needs the internet," I finally felt seen. The business card I'd created with my contact info and newly minted website show-casing my early art and writings was burning in my pocket. After the session, I charged to the front of the room. I tried to explain my story:

Yes, she does! Will you help me get her voice heard? Mother Nature is my client. I don't know how I'm doing it, but I can communicate with the vastness of Source. Multiple dimensions are real. It's complicated! I have messages filled with wisdom for the next generation. The future is not scary, but it will require each of us to be personally invested in the outcome. Can we partner? Will you help me tell the REAL story of the future? Will you help me save the world?

Well, you can guess how that went down. When you are established, you sound wise when you say things like *I have a plan for us to save the world*. When you're a middle-aged woman with zero street cred, you sound nuts.

But I was not to be defeated; a turbocharged quest for in-formation ensued.

Suffice it to say I had always SORTA believed in the *sixth sense*. And as my awakening took hold, I discovered that mine was reasonably evolved. Nothing was really connecting, but I let it flow. To be fair, I didn't know how to stop it.

And once I leaned in, things began to make more sense. After all, time was on my side, and so I spent it exploring a wide range of topics, from the zodiac to gender ideology, from religion to the climate crisis. I read, listened to, and watched movies, books, podcasts, videos, TedTalks, yada yada. Infor-mation came streaming at me 24/7, intuitively and conscious-ly. Sometimes the path took me on a deep dive, sometimes I just went skimming along the surface. I called my process for acquiring seemingly random information *Me University*.

Above all, I was finally connecting to a *knowing* I had been aware of since childhood. A fire within that yearned to pursue possibilities and make them a reality. Now that I was tuning in, I could see the flames had been burning within me for as long as I could remember. As a kid, *Peter Pan* was my favorite story. I wanted to be Wendy, Peter, and Tink. Like them, I wanted to experience amazing adventures and to use magic to create a better reality.

Sure, I played well in the sandbox, but I'd never felt like I fit in. Any attempt to explain this was brushed off as me being overly sensitive. Conversely, I vividly remember a sense of belonging in the book. I understood the lost boys and I imagined I'd be safe with them. *Neverland* felt like home.

As I matured, I was taunted and praised in equal measure for always seeing the magic in situations and people. On a good day, I could get things done, push for social justice, or simply make a gathering lots more fun. On a bad day, I was labeled a Pollyanna and told to go play with my fucking fairies. Eyes would roll. My motives would be questioned.

Throughout my entire life folks, my mother in particular, had also expressed concern about my vulnerability. My sensitive nature was mistaken as a sign of weakness and naïveté. My mother often reprimanded me for crying. She never was able to understand that tears are not only a physical release, like sweating, but are also sacred indicators of *truth*, both painful and joyous. "Dear Abby," I got it a lot. As in:

Dear, dear Abby, why are you so unbelievably naive? Things will never get better. Stay in your lane, take what you can, protect what you've got.

Here's the thing. Now, Me University became my Neverland. I was learning that naïve me wasn't so naive. Turns out my sensitive nature was a gift, one that opened the gateway to my intuition and wisdom. I didn't quite understand the implications, but I was also beginning to see that *fear of not belonging* was driving the isolation and tribalism that had us hurting each other, whether that pain was delivered physically, emotionally, and/or spiritually.

As for what to *do* with all the information bombarding me? I still had no idea. But I wondered, if I kept following these *signs*, maybe something would present itself. And I had to do *something*, because I sure as hell couldn't just stand by and watch my fellow humans continue to treat each other like shit. I wasn't going to let the DMV or anything else get in the way of us nurturing and nourishing each other. My voice was starting to present itself. I couldn't let fear stop me from trying to be part of the solution. Just because I was a middle aged woman without a *credible* resume didn't mean I didn't have a plan to save the world.

This book is my plan. I deserve a better future, and so do you, and we won't get there without each other. Enough of the fucking labels. We are Generation WE. Together WE can create better, and it begins by telling the truth of our history and breaking the cycles of generational trauma. Obviously, I've volunteered to go first.

2
familial hierarchy

Beginning at the beginning, building Generation WE means rebuilding our notions of "family." Since humans are social creatures, we are wired to want to belong. The first place we want to belong is to the folks that brought us into this world, our original caretakers, whomever they may be. We look to them to meet not only our physical needs, but also our emotional and spiritual needs. We look to them to tell us how to *be* in the world, in return for their approval, love, connection, and protection.

The familial grid is a microcosm of our human condition. We function on a larger scale the same way we function personally, and interpersonally, within our familial systems. This means that whatever world we create for ourselves, it will always be an extension of this first grid.

Seems obvious, right? But what's not so obvious are the flaws in the basic structure of the familial grid *as we know it*, and the societal malfunction that results from this. Our family systems are flawed because they assume that hierarchy is the model for human success. But that's not true. A hierarchy is the model for human *victory*, not success. The difference is drastic.

Success is not victory. Success includes failure. Success requires flexibility, experimentation, and vulnerability. Success rejects the binary and allows for infinite possibilities. The foundation for success lies in collaboration. Victory, on the other hand, is all about conquest. And our current familial and societal systems are not set up for success (yet). They are set up for victory.

In a hierarchy, there is a leader at the top. They write the rules. They are also the only ones with the right to challenge or change the rules. A second in command puts the rules into action and keeps things humming along. Everyone else in the group functions under the folks ruling the roost, with hopes that someday they will matriculate into one of the top spots.

As it stands today, *the first place we learn how to belong* is within the patriarchal hierarchy of the familial grid. And by patriarchy, I also mean matriarchy. Matriarchy is patriarchy in a skirt. Both uphold binary thought patterns. Both perpetuate judgment. Both promote perfectionism. Both are responsible for the systemic "othering" that we continue to pass along generational lineages. Both have caused enormous pain to each and every one of us. It's why I've renamed the whole hierarchical system the PAIN-triarchy.

Certainly, the hetero cis-gendered family grid has issues, but the same issues are present in same sex marriages where the familial grid looks like any other hierarchy. A hierarchy is a structure without flexibility. It will say its goal is to provide stability, but *victory, winning,* and being the *best* are really what define its purpose.

Yes, humans are tribal creatures and need other folks to survive. To ensure said survival, the family tree plants its roots and branches out accordingly, adding layers upon layers to the chain of command. Sort of like an army. But wait a minute. Do we need each other to *survive* or do we need each other to *thrive*?

Hear me out.

I believe the pain-triarchal hierarchy of the familial grid is the nucleus of our collective angst, because this structure keeps us trapped in survival mode. Survival mode perpetuates the notion that for me to win, you must lose. Survival mode upholds the notion that some people deserve to love more than others. Survival mode celebrates supremacy—and thus its opposite— subordination. Survival doesn't keep *us* alive, it keeps *some of us* alive. In doing so, each individual's inherent worth is constantly questioned and must be earned or proven.

Who of us is *worthy* of food, shelter, education ... love? Life? Am I? It has taken me sixty years, and likely several lifetimes, to realize the impact of survivalism on my being. When my mother took over the family business at twenty-three, she modeled to me drive and tenacity. If she could single-handedly take on such great responsibilities, so could I. I made it my mission to do my best to follow in her footsteps. The result has been a never ending cycle of feeling like I am never enough, no matter what I do or accomplish.

I was also weaned on white supremacy, and so were you. It is not possible to be a human living today without this being our story. This doesn't make having white skin bad or good. It makes our history with skin color problematic. The same is true of our history with gender. The racial divide and the gender divide bear the weight of our inherited—versus inherent—survivalism. The other divides intersect with alarming consistency. The ableist divide, the class divide, the political divide, the orientation divide, the religious divide, the size divide. The list is long, complicated, and messy.

My existential crisis made me question everything about my identity: as in what it meant to be a straight, cis, white, Jewish, female. And so I went back to the primary source of my learning, my familial grid. I began my investigation by telling the story of us. I mapped it out *Dear Diary* style. The concept of *belonging* was a puzzle I needed to crack. I wrote about my family over and over and over again. Who were we? What had happened to us? Where and when did these events take place? How did these events make us feel?

I focused predominantly on my relationships with my mother and my kids. While certainly other relationships in my life informed the plot line to my story, I carried these three humans at the core of my existence. Little did I know I was actively trying to break a cycle of something for which I had yet to discover the language ... generational trauma.

Before I carry on, I want to pause and explain a bit about my relationship with generational trauma. I am not a scientist nor a therapist. I am speaking strictly as a fellow human who intuitively began to notice a pattern in the survivalist tendencies threaded through our everyday experiences.

I realized that when I felt threatened or unsafe, my actions came from a place of fear, not curiosity. I didn't question why I felt scared, I just reacted. I could see that I wasn't the only one; everyone around me was afraid of something too. It wasn't that our fear was obvious, quite the contrary. Most of us claimed we weren't feeling it at all.

And yet, the undertow of our angst was undeniable, and our reactions to it manifested as follows. I noticed some of us would become opinionated and arrogant, some timid and unsure. Some would yell, blame, and ostracize. Some would withhold love, nourishment, and nurturing. Some would become sullen, smaller, and subservient. Some would become overly agreeable, compliant, and disingenuous. Most of us attached to certain behaviors as a means to escape our fears, such as addictive relationships to food, alcohol, drugs, work, social media, exercise, and excessive material purchases.

All this to say, each of us were reacting to the trauma of being human, because trauma has been normalized as our given state. We have been schooled to recognize that life is unfair and taught that our job is to endure whatever crap comes our way, regardless of how dysfunctional the situation or actions of others may be. Bottom line, *survival is a tactic we have developed for enduring trauma, not healing it*. And how we endure trauma is what has been paid forward.

I would describe my personal trauma as the papercut variety. But from this vantage point I was able to connect the dots between papercuts and severed limbs. Pain was pain and, to varying degrees, the trauma loop was affecting each and every one of us.

That said, I quickly saw that the home I grew up in was a badass matriarchy. My mother was a human tornado who swept everyone who crossed her path up into her one-size-fits-all version of reality. If something didn't fit my mother's vision for how things ought to be, it was unilaterally considered *wrong*. Her views seemed to align more with the world than mine, so I adjusted myself to fit.

Roberta didn't necessarily believe in God, but she sure did believe in traditions and upholding clearly defined gender roles, *Fiddler on the Roof* style. The mammas, the papas, the daughters, and the sons; as defined according to her and served her way. As a result, my concept of gender was really off-base under her tutelage.

My mother didn't believe in the ERA. She was her own wave of feminism. She didn't get all the fuss. In both her belief system and her daily life, she embodied the 1982 Enjoli perfume commercial. She could "bring home the bacon, fry it up in a pan, and never let you forget you're a man."

And it was true. She could raise a blended family, run a business, cater to the elders, and have dinner on the table by six. She was also complex—intuitive, brilliant, generous, cynical, egotistical, and manipulative. My father had one job, and she had *all* the jobs. She never left him for an evening. He never took us kids to a doctor's appointment or cooked a meal.

Thanks to Roberta, our family looked like *The Brady Bunch*. Charming, delightful, funny. You know, "It's the story of a lovely lady ..." Hers included divorcing my biological father. The dad who raised me lost his first wife to breast cancer. The new fam included me, my younger brother, and my three older siblings (they never felt *step*). Our ages ranged from five to sixteen when she and my dad married.

Sure, we had some seemingly *minor* problems, issues with

school, dates, friends, but Roberta could always *save the day*. She seemed to be a combination of Bob, Carol, and Alice of *The Brady Bunch*: the successful father, supportive mother, and wise housekeeper all rolled into one superhuman.

Of course, underneath the facade, the foundation was cracking at the seams. Folks like my mom didn't know how to deal with *trauma*—theirs, or anyone else's. Like a Mack truck, she just kept rolling along.

She was also raised with the philosophy that winners are strong, and losers are weak. Brawn, anger, and resilience equaled strength. Equaled victory and *survival*. Tears, emotions, and vulnerability equaled weakness. She thought shoving her pain, grief, and disappointment under the carpet made it all go away. But it didn't. It just gave these challenging emotions the opportunity to fester and wreak havoc on the rest of us in the form of passive/aggressive behavior and angry outbursts.

As a result, it was difficult for me to know where I stood with her in a given situation. Her temper went from zero to a hundred in a nanosecond. Roberta had an acerbic tongue that could slice you in two with a sentence. Since she gave both her praise and judgment freely, I felt like I was on trial every day. It was confusing.

Roberta and I differed greatly in demeanor. She was harsh, I was gentle. She was analytical, I was empathetic. We intersected in a passionate love for each other. She adored me and I worshiped her. I was her person and I stuck to her like glue. Being Roberta's sidekick was a 24/7 gig.

Together we made a dynamic duo, and people benefited greatly from our union. To our extended family, I was my mother's secretary. I agreed to take on organizing birthdays, celebrations, yada yada. I managed our "family fund," which everyone contributed to annually to keep group gift giving and family events—usually coordinated by me—fairly financed. As for the community at large, I was an active volunteer and often very visible in my efforts. My mother was proud of my achievements and absolutely supported these endeavors.

As she pushed and pulled me in an effort to create me in her ideal image of a woman, I pushed and pulled myself to be my *best* self. By this I mean the version of myself that I hoped was getting it *right* on a deeply moralistic level. Perfectionism for the daily double, anyone?

At the end of the day, Roberta did her best, me too. She also wanted to be the best, me too. However, *best* is a double bind in relation to our humanity. On one hand, it implies that being the best, the victor, the winner, is the point of being human. And on the other hand it again implies that not everyone is equally worthy.

Mom passed away in 2021. Our relationship was complicated and codependent to the end. This does not reflect poorly on either of us. Nor does it detract from the closeness of our relationship and all the wonderful things we shared. It is just an honest assessment of how papercuts keep us trapped in generational trauma. I'm thinking maybe you can relate? The pain-triarchy is currently what structures our reality. And this, my friends, has been instilled into each and every one of us, whether we are aware of its effects or not.

To paraphrase Carl Jung, until WE make the unconscious conscious, it will direct our lives. Thus, our generational trauma will continue to play out until we take a stand to heal it.

My awakening coincided with the last six years of my mother's life. It gave me the chance to begin the arduous journey of making my unconscious conscious. By this I mean I began to intentionally evolve. In doing so, I like to think I was able to kickstart some significant evolution for my mother as well. I know she did for me.

Roberta had a hard time opening the pathway between her head and her heart. Throughout my life, my emotional intelligence was an ability of mine she admired, she just didn't know how to engage it herself. Instead, she settled on being *the kindest bitch you'd ever meet*. While she wasn't able to complete her evolutionary work in this arena with me, I hope I activated a desire for her soul to keep trying in the next life.

For her part, Roberta initiated my departure from the clutches of pain-triarchal perfectionism. Her fire to passionately embrace life was instilled in me, as was the pain caused by her idealism. With my kids I learned how to moderate the volume of that fire within me by leveling up my own evolution. I will be showing you *how* I did this herein.

Roberta certainly played a very active role in my family life; sometimes this was supportive, sometimes it got in between us. Meanwhile, I did my best to establish a different familial grid with my kids. With Roberta and me, the hierarchy was unimpeachable; the *survival* of our family unit depended on it. With them, I made sure things were more fluid between us. Doing so created a much softer environment.

If Roberta was a badass matriarch, then I was a matriarch-lite. Parenting was my domain, and my husband Craig, for the most part, tried to stay out of the day-to-day. Without a *job* pulling at me, I had time on my side to be innovative, attentive, and available to freely explore their feelings and mine. I may have been a softer parent than Roberta, but I was still tied to many of the expectations and judgments of the pain-triarchal playbook. If she was *my way or the highway*, with my kids, I began the process of learning how to establish an *interactive* familial structure. More, *let's create a way that supports each of us to thrive*

I can't claim that I raised my kids free from the pain-triarchy, but I can say I innately understood that it was my job to try to grow with them, as opposed to molding them into an idealized version of me. As such, I learned how to parent *me* in tandem with parenting them. I made our home into an open classroom for both our hearts and minds.

Our relationship was a calm space. We functioned like dancers as we approached the routines of life, both in our emotional responses and in the practicality of chores, meals, errands, activities, school, and social life. Our rhythm together was synchronized and I referred to us as the A-team.

Does that mean we never had problems? Most obviously not. What our environment did provide was a grid with wiggle room: room for vulnerability. Access to vulnerability set the stage for my awakening and enabled us to engage in the deep healing necessary to break through our generational trauma.

3
evolution

I vividly remember the day I took Samantha and Chad to see *Lilo & Stitch*. It was a rainy summer afternoon. The kids were little and I was thrilled to have Disney serving up the day's entertainment. We got our snacks and settled into our seats in the back of the theater. From the minute the opening music began to play, the three of us didn't budge, nor did we utter a peep. We were mesmerized by the story.

I think Chad may even have astral-projected onto the screen and into Stitch's body. He felt alien, even at four. Chad is gay, by the way. Not something he could put into words back then; there was just a *feeling* that he was somehow innately different.

Samantha was a perfect foil for Lilo; me, the older sister, Nani. The concept of chosen family and home resonated deeply for each of us. Lilo's famous quote at the end hit us on a soul level we couldn't put into words:

"Ohana means family, family means no one gets left behind or forgotten."

We sat there as the credits rolled and just sobbed. Tender, ugly, heaving sobs. The theater lights went up and we sat paralyzed in our seats, trying to catch our breath. We remained silent for a bit. I drew them into a tight bear hug and proclaimed THAT'S US. I promised that *we* would always be there for each other.

But why was it that we needed to hear this at our core? After all, we were sitting right there, together, safe and secure. But if Chad had always felt different, Samantha and I felt it too. There was a collective yearning among us for something we didn't yet know, but which we knew we would create together.

***

How this would unfold for the three of us began to become clear during my deep dive into the spiritual realm post-existential crisis. What Samantha, Chad, and I were here to create together, what we saw in the story of *Lilo & Stitch*, would be a crucible of intense growth for us.

Over the course of time, a good amount of our human evolution has been in response to external conditions. Nature ruled our livelihood and religions formed to help us understand the workings of the natural world, including the workings of our humanness, both biologically and psychologically. Our evolutionary path also helped our bodies and actions adapt to keep us alive. To survive.

In contrast, while many are still just trying to survive, the current stage in our evolutionary process is internal, incorporeal, and voluntary. It is about our *thriving*. The focus now is on self-manifestation, not self-preservation. As such, our personal and familial evolution is critical to the evolution of the collective, and vice versa.

Serendipity drew me into a deeper investigation of what this chapter would hold. It was fall of 2019, six months before COVID-19 would turn the world upside down. The hard introspective work of my awakening was starting to pay off. I had made some progress in letting go of my baggage: personal, cultural, and societal. As a result, I felt a bit lighter .

When I woke up one morning with the words "age of Aquarius" embedded in my mind, I was intrigued. I'd always liked the song from *Hair*, but what did it mean? The words came out of nowhere, so of course I googled them.

I learned that the Age of Aquarius has to do with equality among genders, personal freedom, and the activation of divine feminine energy. There is a point of view that offers 2012 as the kickoff for this period, a time when humanity's truth will be revealed, consciousness expanded, and enlightenment will transpire.

Besides the zodiac woo, I realized that the song had been the soundtrack to my life, literally. "The Age of Aquarius" was my father-in-law's favorite song from the show. He gave my husband a framed copy of the album, which hangs on the wall adjacent to my office. We also have the Broadway banner for *Hair* hanging in our basement. My husband purchased it as an ode to his father shortly after his death in 1995.

HAIR: The American Tribal Love Rock Musical

Well then ... here we are.

Tribal love: so that was the goal of this shift from surviving to thriving, beginning with our family systems. And then spreading out to Generation WE.

Looking around me, a shift was definitely presenting.

Some folks have referred to these times as messianic, or apocalyptic. To others, the breakdown of pain-triarchal hierarchies in government, gender, race, and families speaks to an influx of radical love, and concern for the success of WE over the victory of ME. Regardless of the language that works for you, or WTF you think is going on, if we have indeed entered the Age of Aquarius, things appear to be playing out accordingly.

Corruption has been running rampant, the environment is on the precipice of collapse, and a sea of inequality has flooded the planet. But to think that people had it better in other times is a lie.

Better for who?

The dark reality of our situation is that it reflects how shitty we have been to each other going back millennia. But with equal clarity, the path to enlightenment is coming into focus. The pull between the past, the present, and the future is palpable. Everything we thought we knew is up for review. Just because something *was* doesn't mean it was good. A deep scrutiny of our past beliefs and actions is required. The evolutionary potential of these times lies in our perspective, in our shift from the pursuit of victory, to the pursuit of success.

I believe we are also at an impasse in which the *fight-or-flight* instinct is no longer serving us. When in fact, it could destroy us. Moving forward we will need to utilize our intuition (our higher self) to shift to a place of rest-and-digest (the space where we can access our full human potential). Science backs up my claim.

The fight/flight instinct is controlled by our sympathetic nervous system. It activates our adrenaline and prepares our body to be ready to react physically to potential danger. And yes, throwing a punch, screaming, or hightailing it the fuck out of trouble has helped us defend ourselves against nature and each other.

We have relied heavily on this instinct and as a result it is highly developed. The bad news is that it trains our sights on *victory*—because when power accumulates to those in the top spots, we continue to feel threatened by each other. On a less ominous level, our interpersonal relationships have become controlled by the person who can scream the loudest. This is true whether we duke it out verbally or leave because we can't face conflict.

But, what if we could evolve beyond the desire for power over one another? What if we could evolve towards *potential* instead? What if we could all agree that nature was no longer a threat, and that we had, actually, become a threat to nature? What if we wanted all of us to live fuller, richer, calmer lives? Could we make that happen?

Good news! Our bodies equip us with a solution.

The *rest-and-digest* function of the brain is controlled by our parasympathetic nervous system. This pathway restores our body to a calm and composed state of being. Our blood pressure lowers, we catch our breath. In this state, we are able to contemplate and to respond as opposed to react. In doing so, we can make better decisions and build better relationships, because we are no longer in a state of defense.

In short, our bodies come with options when it comes to either surviving, or thriving. While both the sympathetic and parasympathetic nervous systems kick in without our conscious effort, I believe we can also control how we either react, or respond, to environmental stimuli. I believe we can engage the wisdom of our higher self—wisdom learned over lifetimes—to train our minds to respond from a place of calm instead of reacting from a place of fear.

Acting on the wisdom of our highest self, versus just doing it like we always have, is what psychological evolution looks like—and mine began that moment in the theater. Watching Lilo, Stitch, and Nani choose to build a life together against all odds, Samantha, Chad and I intuitively realized that we could create better. But better what?

In the years that followed, I learned that the key to my freedom, and theirs, lay in an understanding of our shackles. After all, we couldn't evolve if we didn't know what we were evolving from. We also couldn't love each other fully until we could, *with abandon*, fully be ourselves.

Becoming ourselves has been as challenging as you would imagine. It has meant expanding our capacity to understand each other by responding with curiosity instead of fear. It has meant learning to digest situations instead of just reacting to them. Let me be clear, this is not an easy feat. Navigating the chaos of being human can be painful. We have found the more we are able to let go of expectations and judgments, the more we are able to step into the power of our potential.

The lyrics of "Aquarius" are weighty when taken with the magnitude they were meant to deliver. They have become the cornerstone to our relationship. *Harmony and understanding, sympathy and trust abounding.* Some days it still goes better than others, but what we have learned most of all, is that we matter.

You matter too. How you are doing matters. What you are doing matters. You are not being asked to single-handedly save the world; your part in our collective evolution is to simply be as YOU as you can be. This means you are being asked to participate in the healing of the generational trauma that is yours to carry. You are being asked to open the pathway between your mind and your heart, between your analytical and intuitive self.

Leading the way for me was the wisdom available from my highest self. It's there for you too, but you have to welcome it in.

4
highest self

I used to believe that we entered the world for a single life-time. I thought every human entered as a blank slate, ready to embrace the world, fulfill a given purpose, and then check out according to that plan. I also believed we came stamped with a bunch of labels, and that our fulfillment of the labels' requirements was part of our job. A job that ideally included the procreation of our species.

I was born a white, Jewish female. So I followed all the rules, got married, had kids, and chose family life over pur-suing a career. I thought this path was my calling, my given purpose. Which ironically proved to be true ... but not in the way I imagined. Turns out my focus on the familial grid be-came the thesis for my wider work, and would be integral to the evolution of my soul. Go figure.

Anyway, my labeling belief system was upended in the summer of 2007. The kids were young, but both were old enough to attend overnight camp. Samantha had been going for a few years, now Chad was finally of age. The camp was part of the network I attended as a kid. I was familiar with the location and felt the environment provided a diverse array of skills that supplemented school and home life. They loved that they got to explore the place of my childhood escapades.

While they were at camp, Craig and I were supposed to be on vacation. We decided to visit Cleveland, since our hometown was also close to camp. The plan was to relax, see friends, and catch up with family, but Craig wasn't in vacay mode. Work had followed him and he was extremely stressed out. He was agitated and on his phone constantly. I empathized with his frustration, but I was frustrated too. We couldn't seem to catch a break. Work and life just got lumped together, seemingly without any time off.

As a result, I was having a literal and figurative bad hair day. I was burnt out and feeling scrappy. I thought a new look could maybe help. I couldn't fix his mood, but I could fix my hair. A few days into our trip, while he dealt with whatever work crisis was stewing, I made an appointment with an acquaintance who owned a salon. That chance encounter led me to the book *Many Lives, Many Masters* by Dr. Brian Weiss.

As she tamed my split ends and colored my roots, she jabbered on and on about the book. The words poured out of her with an intensity that told me she needed me to understand. I *had to* read the book. It was a directive, although she tried to make it sound like a recommendation. Sure enough, the next thing I knew, I was at Barnes & Noble with the one copy they had in my hand.

Well, I couldn't put it down. The book discussed the concept of past-life regression and the soul's continuing ascent in a timeless journey to higher levels of knowledge. I discovered there were specific fields of expertise to be mastered over multiple lifetimes, and that guides ahead of me were leading the way.

The book forever changed the way I viewed the universe and my place in it. It got me thinking about the world differently, but I was still about eight years away from my spiritual nose dive. I had more living to do before I was ready for the full experience.

I now believe that my soul, and yours, is comprised of energy that is not tied to a specific physical form. In other words, I believe my soul is the essence of me. A *me* that transcends time and space.

I also believe our souls are on a mission to create experiences that accrue wisdom: wisdom that is gained both from the human experience, and in the dimensional space *in between* lifetimes. Our souls carry no gender, race, orientation, religion, or size. Therefore, I have been, and will be, everything I need to be to create the experiences that make me exactly me; my soul's many lives intersecting in a unique pattern, kinda like my thumb print. You too.

And while every human being has a soul, that doesn't mean you can't also absolutely be a dick. I'm sure a few folks immediately come to mind. Our history has given us so many great examples. From the political to the personal, even the worst of us has a soul. Just one that's not very evolved.

It helps me to see the evolution of a soul as being like a video game. Each new life is a new level. My soul exists in the player, or avatar (aka body), of my choosing. The me that guides my moves in the game is my highest self (my wisest self). When I've learned what I need to learn, and faced the dragons I need to slay, I get to advance to the next level. But I can't move forward without fully understanding whatever concept is being presented to me.

Taking the analogy further, the skills I learn in the game help me "level up." Just like in a video game, the more I practice, the more I gain a better understanding of how to use them. The same is true of life's lessons. My soul's evolution is cylindrical and the lessons will circle back in the name of mastery. Seen in this light, history *does* repeat itself, but with the express purpose of helping us learn how to do it better.

With any luck, my history levels up with me. As my highest self *responds* better, I create a better reality. *The same is true for you.*

It is important to note here that age and wisdom function differently. Age is linear, wisdom is full-spectrum. True, I become older with each passing year, but unless I choose to evolve I do not become wiser with age. Wisdom increases with experience. This wisdom carries over from life to life. As such, my soul age, my level of evolution, has nothing to do with my chronological age in this life.

For all the young, wise peeps out there, likely someone has referred to you as an *old soul*. What if they mean this literally? Like me, you were probably a very sensitive child. You may have felt the world within and around you very deeply. You may have been told to toughen up. That was a mistake. Your sensitivity is a sign that your sixth sense is reasonably developed and that you have reached a more advanced level in the video game of soul ascension. This does not make you *better* than other folks, it makes you more expansive. The ascension levels are relevant only in terms of helping each other create better.

If we all have a soul, then everyone also has a sixth sense (aka extra-sensory perception). Think gut, intuition, imagination, creativity, serendipity, and inner knowing. Tuning into our sixth sense is how we access our highest self. The highest self is where wisdom accrues. Applying this in the "real world" is a skill set that requires awareness, intention, and practice to cultivate.

This is because greed, inadequacy, and fear impede access to our highest self. They are considered to be functions of lower energy fields, and they trip us up all the time. But this too is part of our evolutionary process. Each time we choose to access our highest self when faced with these demons, we level up our energy field by engaging wisdom and thus creating a more *successful* outcome. Whereas, without wisdom, greed, inadequacy, and fear keep us focused on *victory*.

Are you staying with me here? Let me give you an example of my higher self applying the wisdom of my lived experience to my soul's ascension.

I was about six years into my awakening, when my highest self began nudging me: *did I really like how I felt when I drank alcohol?* It wasn't a moral judgment on the part of my higher self, but it was a flag. I was shocked that my love affair with the grape was being questioned, and by the most unlikely source: me.

I didn't drink excessively, but I did drink consistently. A glass of wine or two was a treat I looked forward to at the end of the day, good or bad. Maybe not every day, but certainly more days than not. Wine had become tied up with emotional release, comfort, control, courage, fun, fear, boredom—the list of associations was endless.

I doubled down on my attachment to wine during the emotional upheaval of COVID-19, which coincided with the demise of my mother's health. I was being challenged in a way I had never been challenged before; I was at my wit's end, but I was also more aware of my behavior than I had ever been. I began noticing that when I drank, my tongue would become loose and my emotions were displayed more transparently than I was comfortable with. I grew paranoid the next day as to what had come out of my mouth.

I was with my siblings the day of my last drink. It was a few months after our mom had died. Emotions were understandably running high. We had unfinished business between us, and I was deep in my grief. The first night of our reunion, the wine flowed. But it failed me; I was a wreck. I felt out of control and went to bed feeling like shit.

I couldn't sleep. My highest self kicked into high gear, and led me to my iPad. I spent the night researching the concept of *sober curiosity*. What was it? Did I want to give it a try? Apparently it was a one day at a time kind of deal. I could practice not drinking ... and answer my question—*do I like I how I feel when I drink?*—for myself.

The next morning, I committed to giving it a whirl. It was coincidentally (or not) July 4th. A memorable moment for my independence from alcohol. The day was dicey, filled with intense family dynamics, but I held my ground. It was a brave move. I felt all the feelings, but with the confidence of clarity. No substance to make anything seem better or worse; it was what it was.

By listening to the instructions of my highest self, I have never felt better. I can have a drink anytime if I so choose. Nothing bad will happen. But for me, it's more than likely that nothing good will, either. The attachment pushes all my buttons, because my soul has learned that my insecurities can be triggered by the grape.

Also, that I'm just as witty, brazen, silly, and goofy without alcohol in the mix. The difference is I'm in control of how I feel, and that feels good, even when I'm sad, angry, frustrated, or depleted.

As for how this lesson applies to the subject of soul ascension? In my next life, I hope I am able to carry forward the benefits of sitting with my emotions, instead of avoiding them with distractions. Being present with the emotions that reside in me helps me slow down and digest a situation before I react.

Let's take a minute to imagine a world where we all tried to live according to the instructions of our highest self. A self, that is, that has access to the wisdom of lifetimes. No age restrictions, no hierarchies, just humans (and souls) collaborating to create better.

We would care for each other and ourselves with great consideration because we would understand that we are all interconnected, and that our future is dependent on our shared welfare.

We would work together to find ways to end poverty and homelessness because we can— because food, housing, and healthcare are basic human needs, and because we know that we have the shared resources to meet them.

We would prioritize ways to address mental health and

mental well-being, because we would have learned that WE will not survive if ME is in despair.

We would ensure the rights of all humans in regards to their bodies and their choices, because we would each have learned that body autonomy is an inalienable right. Period.

We would fix the broken educational systems, and we would treat teachers and students with respect, because we would have learned that education is the key to our collective success.

We would also make higher education fucking free, because we would know learning is fundamental to creating a vibrant society. If it is only reserved for a select few, our society remains stagnant and stripped of potential because all of our talents are not represented.

We would close the political divide and actually collaborate on solutions that are in the best interest of the people, because our experiences over many lifetimes would have reminded us that we ARE the people.

We would care deeply about our planet, because we would realize that this is the only place we have to live, over lifetimes, for all eternity. We wouldn't want to trash our planet, because we wouldn't want to trash humanity.

Most of all, if we lived according to the instructions of our highest self, I believe it would remind us, daily, that we are more than enough, just as we are. And if we were all living from this place, we would all be able to express our truest selves without fear of being ridiculed, ostracized, maimed, raped, tortured, taunted, or killed.

This in turn would enable us to create freely in all fields. Humanity has so many untapped talents. The reason we can't access them, or develop them, is because most of us spend our lives just trying to survive. Aiming for victory, instead of collaborating on success.

Am I just dreaming, or can WE really create better?

I know we can, but we have to do the work of readdressing our labels, dismantling the hierarchies that created them, and healing from the trauma that has ensued. Here goes.

5
jewish white female

Until 2020, I honestly didn't identify as white. Yes, it was the box I checked for race, but this is only because following World War II, it has been inappropriate to formally acknowledge Jewish as a race. I didn't feel white and was treated by the world accordingly. I was a *Jewish* American, not a regular American. I was part of the tiny minority presumably responsible for the death of Christ; my skin color was irrelevant. I wasn't Christian. I was an outsider.

BTW, Jewish skin color is a point of interest. Judaism is a religion, not a race. Given our predominantly Eastern European history, many American Jews have white skin. But there are Jewish people all over the world, including in the US, with a multitude of different skin colors.

Anyway, the disparity between skin color and class was (and still is) a chasm of phenomenal magnitude and being Jewish just added another layer of complication to the mix. We were white-*ish*, so we did not face the same subjugation as BIPOC folks, but we were still segregated.

White folks didn't want to live alongside "our kind." I

grew up in a neighborhood that was ninety-three percent Jewish and probably ninety-seven percent "white." My family was part of the uprising of Jewish affluence and we lived in one of the smaller homes in the older section of town. Yes, *separate but equal* applied to Jews too. Until the Fair Housing Act of 1968 we couldn't live on the street behind us, it was restricted. No Jewish people. No Black people. I'm sure others were barred too. Basically, you could only live there if you were white and Christian.

For our part, we created our own communities, social clubs, and schools. There was inverse segregation in this impulse, too. My dad had fought in World War II, an experience which became tied to our task to "never forget." We were to marry Jewish, support Jewish causes, keep Jewish customs alive. The idea was to protect our own ... because no one else would.

From a young age, I also found myself trying to come to terms with my parents' prejudices. The very people who instilled in me their support for the progresses of the Civil Rights Movement would just as quickly deem another inferior for actions, behaviors, and situations they knew nothing about. They were working hard to achieve a better position on the hierarchical ladder to acceptance. To victory, even. At the top, were the white, Christian, heterosexual, cis males. I believe it was self-protection that kept my folks from realizing that the prejudices they maintained mirrored the prejudices projected against them. Against us.

I was just a kid with a heart. I remember watching Martin Luther King's "I have a dream" speech in middle school. Tears streamed down my face. When the film was over I realized I was the only one crying. As usual. Be it on the playground, reading a book, or watching a movie, I felt every injustice as if it was my own. I had a passion for *equality*. As I learned more about American history, I was certain I was becoming wiser and more broad minded than my folks. By my teenage years I prided myself in thinking any racism they displayed had nothing to do with me.

And yet. When I decided I wanted to be friends with a girl on my high school dance team who was biracial, I was told by my parents I could be friend*ly*, but that a friend*ship* was unacceptable. They believed her folks engaged in *antisocial* behavior. If her folks' *morals* were so *liberal* to allow a white person to love a Black person, what other *outrageous* acts would they allow their daughter to be involved in?

You know when you meet someone and you just click? That's how I felt when I met her and I wanted to get to know her better. I wish I could say I fought for that friendship, but I didn't. I acquiesced. Shame on me. But my parents could be harsh, and I wanted to keep my ass out of trouble. It was a small infraction; only I knew the whole story, and we remained friendly acquaintances. But in the context of xenophobia, my parents' intervention and my complicity in this was hideous.

Today this would be labeled a "microaggression," just one more brick added to the walls that divide our shared humanity. These microaggressions are kryptonite to Generation WE. *To each their own* is not fine. Prejudice is not fine. Segregation is not fine. Labeling anybody this or that based on the color of their skin is not fine. Period.

I also know what it feels like to be on the receiving end of these microaggressions. For example, my kids' educational environment was predominantly white Christian. While the school attempted diversity, the playground could sometimes be rough. *Boys will be boys* and some ridiculous game of 8th grade tag revolved around *kill the Jew*. It was squashed, but it happened.

Every time the headlines read *antisemitism is on the rise*, fear pulses through my body. My community stands on high alert. And by community, I mean Jews locally and globally. We look for the signs; *are we here again*? A shooting in a synagogue in France affects us the same as if it happened down the street. Holocaust-related imagery seeps into our collective memory. We hold each other, literally and figuratively. We utter, *and this is why we can never forget*.

I share all this information to explain why recognizing that I was *white* confounded me. I never felt white, because I wasn't the right kind of white. And then the events of 2020 made the benefits of my white*ish* privilege resoundingly clear. I was crushed by the implications of any harm I may have caused, albeit from naïveté.

It was Chad who really schooled me in my privilege. From high school on he would try to explain that I had to broaden my lens past antisemitism and realize how many barriers my skin color walked me through. These interactions were laying the foundation for my understanding of my role in enacting Generation WE. I was an attentive student. Still, I didn't totally get Black Lives Matter until the death of Breonna Taylor. I wasn't paying attention.

Breonna was a twenty-six-year-old Black medical worker who was shot and killed by police officers here in Louisville on March 13, 2020. The police raided her apartment, shooting her eight times in her own house while she was asleep.

This was my city! My heart simply shattered, and in my grief I focused on what my Black peers were saying. Some were friends, some local social justice advocates, all comrades in creating better. Until this moment I truly was unaware that Black folks were treated differently by the police than white folks. I didn't know that one of Samantha's friends wore his identification badge at all times on campus to ensure the police knew he was a med school student at the University of Louisville and not a threat. There was so much I didn't know.

Equal parts horrified and inspired, I picked up books that clearly were required reading and began following many local and national activists on social media. I knew what it felt like to be the *other* in America, but at the same time, my white skin had protected me from the worst of our history in this country. I felt blind. I felt uneducated. I felt embarrassed. I felt devastated. How had I missed what was going on?

Things were most definitely not fine; things were awful.

I knew I had to evolve but would quickly learn I couldn't shift one part without shifting all of me. My evolution had to be intersectional, and it continued to come in small waves, as each piece of me was splayed on the table for my investigation.

6
she/her

I distinctly remember the day it all clicked and I realized that the #MeToo Movement was for me, too. Not because I had been sexually assaulted, but because I finally connected the dots: it was because of my gender that I was and always had been treated as inferior to men. It was 2019, and I had launched a monthly art series inspired by Pantone, entitled "Color Me ..." The month was May, and the color on deck was Blue Iris, "Color Me Deep."

A hit song by my recording artist high school friend Marc Cohn, "Dig Down Deep," played on loop in my head as I worked on my piece. The day after I completed it, I woke up pissed! This level of anger was unfamiliar to me, and it seemed to have come out of nowhere. Luckily I had a therapy session booked for the same day.

For the record, my version of therapy in this regard refers to my practice of energetic healing with a person who works with crystals. Serendipity brought us together as part of my awakening. In the beginning I went once or twice a month. In the last few years I've increased to weekly sessions (except when COVID-19 prevented us from being together). The practice is akin to talk therapy. It's my form of meditation, my catalyst for deep healing, and the springboard for my creativity. My kids have experienced my practice, but they have benefited greatly in working with a psychologist who has become our family therapist.

Anyway, my healer validated and prodded my anger. Why was I so mad? Finally, it came pouring out of me. I could barely catch my breath. The misogyny I'd experienced my entire life spilled out in an ocean of previously unspoken resentment. I was furious that I had chosen raising a family over pursuing a career. I was furious I felt I *had* to choose. I was furious that doing both was not all it was cracked up to be. I was furious picking one over the other wasn't all it was cracked up to be either. I was furious that women were taken advantage of no matter what they did, or how they did it. I was furious with white cis men in general, because it seemed to me that they got it all, while everyone else struggled.

By the end of the session, I was having a very difficult time deciding if I even *liked* being female. Funny coming from me; I had spent most of my life trying to be some version of the *ideal* woman. I spent a good amount of time blaming my mother for my feminine identity crisis. *She* was the reason I didn't understand feminism. It was *her* fault I had abandoned my career. *She* was the one who upheld misogyny with her fucked up adherence to the traditional gender binary.

Or was that all me? Either way, Roberta had been my blueprint for womanhood, and if I wanted to understand who I was and who I wanted to become, I would evidently have to go back and review exactly who she was to me.

What mattered most to me was her approval; as noted, my survival depended on it. If my siblings found other survival tactics, that's their story. They would taunt me that I was *little Roberta*. But that wasn't true. My story is that I just wanted *not to be in trouble*, which meant being the Abby *I thought* she wanted me to be.

Yet, upon review, maybe I needed to see a broader picture. She was a "tomboy," I was the kid who refused to wear pants to preschool. I didn't care if I got dirty, but I preferred not to. I loved my dresses. Yes, fine, I was a priss. Not a compliment, but also not something that has anything to do with the fact that I have a vagina. I was a priss because I liked things organized, neat, and color coded. That's just the nature of me. It's how I think, and it's how I see things. It's how I digest and control the world within and around me.

Control. That was a real issue between my mother and me. She wanted to control everything, which could make me feel very *out* of control. And so in an effort to control something, I handed over the reins to her. If we truly bonded over anything, it was perfectionism. I loved an A-grade, and she just loved to win.

My mother was not academic, I was. She went to Ohio State and dropped out after freshman year. I went to the University of Michigan and graduated with a finance degree. It was a compromise. She wanted me to be an accountant, a skill she felt would serve me if I *needed to work* once I got married.

She also one hundred percent believed the greatest achievement of her lifetime, and her purpose as a woman, was raising children. I believed this too. That was then, not now. Please note that bringing new humans into the world is merely one of the zillions of ways we humans create. Marriage, children, career—these are all just options for growth paths. There is no one *correct* path. We are always creating and I'm done valuing procreation above all other creation. It's absurd.

Back in the day, she couldn't have kids without being married (also absurd), and so that is what she wanted for me. In fairness to her, she didn't just want me to get a MRS. She was a career woman herself. She wanted me to know myself and realize my talents before I tied the knot. She felt she got married too young to my biological father.

My finance degree opened onto a short lived career in banking that led to one in commercial construction, and I spent some time in DC honing my skills. At twenty-eight I moved back to Cleveland. The beltway had become annoying. Plus, by now I was ready to find a husband and settle down.

I found a new position easily. The Cleveland Jewish community was, and probably still is, close knit. Everyone knew everyone, and the idea of welcoming a nice Jewish kid back home to participate and hopefully procreate was very desirable. Also, I had become skilled as a project manager of interior construction, bringing rare (at the time) gender diversity to a field dominated by men.

I joined a real estate conglomerate. The owner and his son-in-law manned the top. Almost everyone was Jewish and male except me, a sole leasing agent, and, you guessed it, the support staff. This made Roberta proud; her girl was a badass. I was playing in the big boys' league, just like her. Mom was a tough cookie, and she loved that her sensitive kid who refused to wear pants could be as ballsy as her.

In her words, the best combination for a woman was to have both brains and a "subtly sexy" appeal. I was literally instructed by her and my male bosses to think of my femininity as my greatest asset, a secret weapon to be deployed as needed for me to make my way in the world. I should *bat my eyes* and be *dumb as a fox*. It wasn't exactly *sleep your way to the top* kind of advice; rather, it was expected that people would underestimate me because I was a woman.

I was to play dumb, then zap 'em with my brains and make them think it was their idea all along. More of the same old crap that had maintained the pain-triarchal gender binary from the beginning of time. The brains behind the throne, the wind beneath their wings. Mom didn't care how she, I, or anyone else for that matter, got power; power was the point for her. If you had it, then you could use it to meet your goals, whether that was to climb the corporate ladder and/or marry well.

If she wanted anything for me, it was this. I was schooled to gain power, and to then use that power to create a powerful next generation. My mother felt that being a woman gave her *all* the power cards. She could be tough as a man *and* soft as a woman. Well, kinda soft. She was a huge flirt, but docile was not in her vocabulary.

Men simply weren't as smart or as resourceful as her. She didn't think anyone was as smart or as resourceful as her. Often this was true, the woman was brilliant. But for brilliance to become wisdom it had to include empathy, and that was much more difficult for her to access. All to say, Mom was a player and she was schooling me to be one too.

My biggest obstacle to *victory* meanwhile, was Maury, an older architect assigned to my projects. He was demeaning, demanding, uncooperative, and unkind. One day the entire team was called to the conference room to discuss some concerns regarding our largest project. It was eleven men and yours truly. Maury threw me under the bus, and blamed me for the project being delayed. Of course, he was the one holding things up by questioning every light fixture and electrical outlet on my plans. Tears of frustration began to trickle down my face.

The owner of the company called me out, "you're crying, just like a woman." Infuriated, I stood up, leaned over the table, intentionally stuck out my chest, and retorted, "I trust this isn't the first time you noticed." It was a badass move for sure. Everyone was taken aback by my candor and chutzpah.

The owner was a *big* deal. He'd spent some time in prison, taking a hit for his team with some tax thing. The buck stopped with him. Loyalty and morality were defined by his rules and he was revered not only within the company, but also among the Jewish community. No one talked back to him without one of two things happening: getting canned or earning his respect.

I earned his respect that day. But, of course, I was still a woman, and I still had to play by his rules. So I did. I batted my eyes and flattered Maury. I patiently answered his unnecessary questions and asked him to explain things to me I already understood. In return, Maury stopped being a schmuck and revised the plans the way I needed him to. He cooperated with me once he didn't feel threatened by me. Eventually, we even became friends.

At the time I thought of this as a win, but in retrospect, misogyny won. Balance was only restored once I abided by the rules. Oh, sure it was *sexy* to have a young, smart, woman on the team, as long as I could smile cute, flatter the men, *and* get the job done. I accepted this was just the way things worked.

Up until that moment in May, the moment my art asked me to *Dig Down Deep*, I actually believed all that *Men are from Mars, Women are from Venus* crap. Now, I found myself questioning my sanity for having bought into such BS. Assigning gender to personality traits is inaccurate, confusing, and wrong. Men and women are not inherently different, and I was exhausted living in a society that claimed we were.

Men, don't you dare sit down. Your reproductive rights are not currently being rolled back. You are not defined by your marital status. "Miss, Mrs, Ms": you are always just a "Mr." Family or career is not a choice you have to make; it's given that you can have both. No one refers to you as a "working dad," you are just a man with a family.

Also, you need to listen because the gender divide has caused you pain too. Middle-aged men make up 70% of suicides. The pressure to succeed, to provide, to "be a man" is enormous.

I'm clearer now on my feelings about being female. It was my guts on my healer's table that day, not Roberta's. It is on me to cultivate awareness about the confines of the gender binary, and to enact my own evolution in this realm.

7
boxed in

And what if you're queer? Are you allowed to have a family? Are you even allowed to *exist*? When your genitalia does not match your gender expression, what planet do you come from then?

One figure who taught me about the necessity of staying true to oneself when this is the case is my first husband. He was a caterpillar trapped in a box provided by the pain-triarchy, and so was I. Let's call my ex, X. X was good looking, refined, worldly, smart, funny, kind, and Jewish. The best part? His family was committed to *tikkun olam* (world repair) and had the means to make a significant impact. What's not to fall in love with?

We met during the Maury era. I had just moved back from DC and a mutual friend wanted to play matchmaker. We all had attended the University of Michigan, but X and I didn't know each other. The mutual friend dragged us both to a U of M Alumni club gathering. Now we were on each other's radar.

The friend was excited about the connection and the three of us formed a tight bond. We joined a number of young professional organizations and invested our time supporting

Cleveland's renowned arts and theater establishments. Yuppies. I can't lie, we had fun making it onto the Cleveland scene and being seen. We danced, not infrequently, in the society pages.

X's family was wealthy, and his folks were a power couple. His oldest brother was a doctor and gay, in a committed partnership (no legally recognized same sex marriage back then). Their relationship was loving and very supported by the family. The middle son, not yet married, had some health issues and was in the family business, as was X.

And so the stage was set. The dream was to hand the reins of the company to X, the logical candidate to carry on his parents' power couple torch. It was a nice dream and I arrived on cue. Our interests were shared and we clicked. Other than the lack of *sexy*, everything was perfect! I'd had sexy and I didn't need it.

Meaning I was pretty much over sex. I was in my late twenties and was tired of the mating and dating game. The act itself had lost a good amount of appeal due to the fact that I just wanted to be settled down. I didn't want any more partners, what I wanted was *a* partner. A best friend. A father for the children I desperately wanted to have. He didn't have to be good in bed, he had to want kids. He had to be nice to me. We had to have fun together. It wouldn't hurt if he was easy on the eyes. X checked all the boxes.

On the side, many hush-hushed me. *X is gay*. It infuriated me. I can't stand when folks hush-hush about someone's sexuality. Oh, he likes the theater, he's gay. Oh, he's a bit effeminate, he's gay. Oh, he's not talented in sports, but would rather read, he's gay. Oh, he likes fashion, definitely gay. Obviously not true, but so it was.

In looking back, I realized many of my *friends* were queer, although most of them not openly. *Out* was not common in the 1980s, but outsiders found each other—and while not queer myself, I surely felt like an outsider. The BS about *boys will be boys* and *girls will be girls* made my skin crawl. I was odd, quirky, artistic, soulful, and sensitive. I wasn't a part of any pack, although I could make it look like I was.

In reality, I had always been Dorothy in search of the Emerald City. I had intuitively sought out folks who wanted to just *be* without strict adherence to all the labels. I found camaraderie with those who, like me, felt a bit out of step with the rest of society. To be clear, I wasn't *far* out there, just a few steps off the beaten path. This was where I found the beauty, kindness, humor, brilliance, and wisdom that felt like *home*.

X spoke my language and I loved him. But, the hush-hush proved to be true, and we didn't get my suburban happily ever after.

The signs were many. I ignored them all and I'm glad I did. The not *sexy*. The honeymoon moodiness. The magazines filled with images of buff men hidden under our bed. But if he was gay, it was not necessarily a deal breaker for me. I would have stayed married. I just wanted to raise a family with him.

But our union was unnatural for him. It was a lie for him. We crashed because of what being gay and in the closet did to X. His closet was extra claustrophobic as he was also being groomed to take over the family business; this was a job for a straight man with a lovely wife by his side. The pressure to be the golden boy was intense.

Within a month of our marriage, X was diagnosed with chronic fatigue syndrome. He couldn't get out of bed, and he rarely went to work. I'd come home and he would be in his bathrobe. Luckily, it was a family business and so he couldn't get fired. He still got paid as if things were normal and I still had my job at the real estate company. There were doctors upon doctors, including a psychologist for both of us. As the months went by and my intuition stepped up its game, I pleaded with X to tell me his truth. I promised to stay; we would face this together. But he couldn't do it. At the time he couldn't tell me he was gay.

Sure, his brother was gay, but he must have felt that was different. I don't know if his family knew he was gay or not, I just know the pressure he was under was enormous. I do know they hoped he'd take over the business. I know they hoped he'd have a family of his own.

Thus, we even tried to procreate, but not with much enthusiasm. For me, my cycle was wonky, and we even tried some infertility drugs. But what tiny slice of a sex life we had prior to getting married disintegrated quickly after we tied the knot. I wasn't mad, I was sad. So very, very sad. Who wants to see someone they love become a sliver of their former self, and lose all of their zest for life?

It became clear to X and me that we were unsustainable. The pressure to perform. The parental expectations. The judgment of society-at-large. The list was long, and it destroyed his health. I watched him crumble beneath the weight of it. We cried and we cried, and we were divorced within our first year of marriage.

I left with the shirt on my back and a small savings account from my job. Legally, I could have asked for a substantial divorce settlement. But that wasn't why I married X. I also left with Hester Prynne's scarlet "A" for "adulterer" etched on said shirt; I didn't cheat, but somehow our divorce was viewed as a betrayal on my part. I couldn't tell folks he was gay, because he hadn't come out yet, and leaving him because of his ill health would be a degradation to the vows I had just recited: "*In sickness and in health ...*"

But what could I do? If I stayed, we were trapped. If I left, I was screwed, but at least we would be free of a burden we couldn't resolve. So I took the hit and moved on. I never outed him. I just tried to walk away with as much dignity as I could muster.

We divorced through arbitration. He asked for my engagement ring back. It was a pricey rock. Against the advice of counsel, I handed it over. His mother told him he would someday give it to the person he *really* loved. No one wanted that for him more than me. He also got the friends, the CDs, the books, the apartment, and the art. I got some kitchen stuff and a broken heart.

I wished he could have just been gay. *Openly gay* for the folks in the cheap seats. Like the way I am openly heterosexual. I wished he could have had the family he so desperately wanted *and* the visibly successful career he'd been promised. Why was he only allowed all this with me as his copilot? He did go on to marry, a man. But only after many years of struggle and the passage of the Equal Marriage Act in 2015.

For my part, I still had a lot of evolving to do. It would be another two decades before I would begin to understand the full implications of X's journey. My perspective back then was more aligned with that of the pain-triarchy than I would like to admit. I didn't have any idea of what it really felt like to be queer, to feel like my sexual impulses were in any way wrong, to feel like I couldn't have a family.

I would learn very intimately how devastating this felt. Ahead lay the understanding that every microaggression is just as damaging as all-out war, because these kinds of paper cuts place us at war with ourselves. Maybe you already understand this. If you don't, I hope by the end of this book you will.

Generation WE is vested in our ability to freely be who we really are in the full vibrancy of all our colors. Only then will our humanity be able to meet its limitless potential.

8
finding out

When I split with X, I could not have imagined I would see another person, let alone my own child, challenged by having been placed in the same box. But in the years that followed, my family remained tethered to the quest for the "ideal," an intergenerational survival mechanism my son and I would have to break.

Following my divorce, I was back in the dating and mating game. I would have to start from scratch. I had married X in June of 1990, and I was married again to Craig in April of 1993. Whoosh, right?

By then, I was thirty-two and pretty anxious to have children. I knew from my brief encounters with X that it would be no easy feat and that infertility intervention would be required. One round of artificial insemination, one miscarriage, one round of IVF, and by 1998 I had two kids. I was lucky.

But the process itself was anything but easy. Besides the costs, the hormones made me feel like crap, and so did being pregnant. I was nauseous throughout my entire pregnancy with Samantha and I just didn't love how my body felt with

Chad. It all felt like a yucky science project. But the intense desire to have kids kept me afloat. Simply put, I desperately wanted to experience parenthood. Why does someone feel drawn to be a doctor? I felt drawn to parenthood with a similar passion.

Anyway, by the time they got here, I was thrilled. I was a *mom*. I was a parent. I honestly can't explain the profound effect this had on me. More than wanting a family, I felt like I had found my calling.

When Samantha arrived, I was relieved. I understood "girl," or so I thought. A few years later Chad entered the world. I was equally thrilled, but I was nervous. I didn't really understand "boy," or so I thought.

Clearly, I was still very trapped by the rules of the pain-triarchy, but my empathetic nature left the door open for growth. I intuitively understood untethered love. This is what held my family together as the challenges of being human played out for each of us, with Chad's queerness leading the way.

While he reached for a book, other boys, and *even* girls, *even* his sister, reached for the ball. When Samantha wanted to play softball, I straight up asked her not to. Chad was struggling with t-ball and I didn't want her to show him up, or emasculate him. She was eight, he was five. His departure from traditional masculinity was slight enough to be smoothed over, but noticeable enough to sometimes get him labeled *gay* on the playground.

This would have happened regardless of his sexuality. The taunt was linked to his general disinterest in sports; he wasn't great at them and frankly didn't give a shit. By nature he was gentler than his peers. Note to all, being gay has nothing to do with your athletic abilities or your interest books. Thank you Carl Nassib (NFL, gay) and John Green (author, straight).

Anyway, he was an inquisitive kid who found wonder in everything. Milo from Atlantis was his alter ego. I loved his curiosity and fueled it with great passion. His ingenuity escalated as he got older. I just tried to add a ball to the mix. If only he could throw it, we would all be fine. How else could he meet his destiny, a Jewish Kennedy?! Yes, I know, deeply flawed on so many levels, but so it was.

Chad had (and has) immense charisma and innate leadership qualities (without the side of misogyny). From the playground to the camp cabin to the classroom, everyone marveled at his ability to infuse morality into the fray of adolescence without being perceived as judgmental. In high school he won the Cementum Award three years out of four. His affable nature brought forth an atmosphere of camaraderie and class spirit. He had the respect and affection of both his teachers and his peers. He was friends with everyone, even though he often felt like an island. Top of his class, charming, handsome, funny, kind, yada yada. What's not to love?

Chad told me he was bi his sophomore year in high school. I held him as he sobbed while I let the tears run freely down my face. I told him it was normal. I told him about X and my friends from college, some of whom had even gone on to become famous.

But, I cautioned, it was a difficult road. If he was *lucky* enough to be bi ... could he practice with girls and see if he could avoid dealing with guys? Could he wait until college before he *officially came out*?

For you can see, I also misunderstood bi. Could he choose a woman and not a man? If he chose a man, of course we would love him, but I worried he wouldn't be able to have a family of his own. I had been to this rodeo.

Oh shit, I had to tell my son he wouldn't be able to have a family!

In the meantime, I cheered Chad on as he went on dates and to dances with "girlfriends," only to find myself prodding a tight-lipped version of him at the end of the night.

Me, with enthusiasm: "Geez, she's really cute! Did you all have fun? You looked so great together ..."

Chad, humoring me: "Yeah, Mom, it was fine. But she (add any number of reasons why he didn't like her). She's just not my type."

Me, still trying: "But, what about (add just one reason I'd hoped he would like her)."

Chad, exhausted and deflated: "Seriously, just friends. I'm really tired. Feel kinda shitty. Going to bed."

I didn't know until much later how much the "family" comment hurt him. I thought by warning him, I was protecting him. I was worried for his future and his safety. This worry was not unfounded; homophobia is real and he had already been touched by it. Mostly it was verbal jabs, but they hurt.

And it was directed at me, too. Chad was class president, and at graduation he delivered a killer speech. He wasn't *out* then, but ya know, the whole *hush-hush* thing. At one of the after parties, a parent came up to me and joked, "Who knew a f****t could be so talented."

I think he thought he was being funny.

Nothing funny about it! Once Chad was officially *out*, it

was not uncommon for a friend to offer their condolences. *How was my husband taking it? We were all so brave*. I was in my ex-in-law's shoes; two decades later, and nothing had changed.

Chad slowly morphed from a confident young man to one riddled with anxiety. In the summer following high school, deeper traces of sadness emerged, informed by the horrific massacre of LGBTQ+ people at Pulse Nightclub in Orlando in June of 2016. It was one of the worst mass shootings by a single gunman in US history, killing 49 people and injuring 53 more.

Chad was living at home at the time. It was supposed to be a carefree summer before college. The pressure of his high achievement life had caught up to him and I hoped he would take advantage of a much needed break. But, alas, the trauma was real.

Truth be told, I didn't think Chad would take it that hard. An interesting response, since I was the one who worried when he put the pride flag on his Instagram, as many did, out of respect. Would folks think he was gay? *Was he safe*? The *hush-hush* had followed him, but at the time, it was still only me who knew his truth. Fear, protection, and denial absolutely consumed me, while I tried to keep things *normal* and move on.

Chad started to show less interest in things, except for his long walks at the gym. With the start of his first semester in college, the mile counts and lists of anxieties he would share with me continued to stretch, as his face thinned and hollowed with each new photo he sent. By his winter break, he was becoming unrecognizable, not least to himself.

I recognized the signs of an eating disorder. I had flirted

with a case of binge eating disorder when I was around Chad's age too. Given our shared passions for food and well-being, it's odd that we both traversed this path, but so it was. I had him start to log his calories, and his weight stabilized; extremely thin, but not dangerously so. His emotional instability, on the other hand, was concerning. By the middle of Chad's second semester, not a week would go by without him sobbing on the phone. He felt useless, ugly, and unlovable. It felt like he was in grief.

Every accomplishment he worked towards became a burden in the rear view, if not an utter failure. Every new project or upcoming event became an obstacle too big to face head on. He would spend hours typing in his room, getting A-grades, but barely eating. My concern for him was overwhelming. I was here again, and it was even worse than with X. Chad was on the edge. I couldn't lose him. I begged him to stay.

What I didn't realize yet was that *I was the one who would have to evolve*. That I would have to uproot my pain-triarchal conditioning about gender and own my vulnerabilities if I was going to be able to provide the care and protection Chad needed.

I was a few years into my awakening by now, and had spent a good amount of time in therapy, reckoning with how my concepts of gender were informed by both my whiteness and my Jewishness. Each session was a deep inquiry into my original existential angst. Into what it even meant to fucking be human.

I found myself asking: why do heterosexual folks get their love applauded and queer folks get their love crucified? How come some of us have to hide the exact same thing that gets others placed on a pedestal? Who deserves a family? A career? Healthcare? Education? Housing? Which human labels came with a get out of jail free card, and why? Was it one's race, class, gender, religion, or orientation? Was choice really free in America, or were our choices predetermined by all of the above?

The answers to my questions were the questions in and of themselves. Society had schooled me to believe that things were black and white. I was beginning to see that society was wrong. To move forward, I realized I needed to get comfortable with the uncomfortable. Conforming to the pain-triarchy was all I knew, and extrapolating oneself from its clutches is excruciating. Not least because it meant acknowledging the ways I had been complicit in my own son's pain.

And there it was. I could see it plain as day. *I* was the reason he always felt unsure. *I* was the reason he wanted so badly to get it *right*. *I* was the double bind in his life. This wasn't about being gay, per se, it was about *idealism*. That is: the notion that there is an ideal way to be a man, woman, human.

Shit. It was my mom and me on rinse and repeat. She'd tried to shape me to be her *ideal woman*; I wanted him to be the *ideal man*. Her dreams and ambitions were wrapped up in my story, and mine were wrapped up in his. Both Team Food Chain and the story of X and I had followed the same plotline.

You could call it the "golden thread syndrome." X, Chad, and I, were all seekers of the gold star for *good* behavior. We sought to embody the traits that received all the coveted As, as in accolades, affirmation, acceptance, and approval. We'd learned that embodying the *ideal*—rather than us being ourselves—is what would ensure we'd always belong, that we'd always be safe. Climb a mountain, climb into a cage, whatever it took to win acceptance, approval, safety.

This is why perfectionism (aka idealism) is one of the pacts of the pain-triarchy. I had watched helplessly as this poison had nearly destroyed X. And yet, unaware of the ways it existed in me, now I had passed it on to the very person I wanted to protect the most from its influence.

9
body parts

Samantha, on the other hand, didn't hit any of my evolution-ary hot buttons. Nor did she seem to require the same fierce protection as Chad. It was like the universe delivered her with a tag on her toe: *with this one, practice what you know*. And so, we winged it, together. And what my higher self had apparently already learned about "girl," was patience and empathy.

Each day together provided the two of us a ticket on Jerry Seinfeld's roller coaster of life: *our hair got messed, we were usually out of breath, and just tried not to throw up*.

Literally. Samantha has spent a good part of her life feel-ing nauseous. She has some autoimmune issues that are ex-acerbated by stress. This manifested as food intolerances as a kid that expanded to thyroid disease in adolescence, PCOS in her early twenties, and most recently an ADHD diagnosis.

Bodies are bodies, yet we've been taught to treat them as if they function robotically. Well, guess what? That doesn't work, for anybody. The survivalism of the pain-triarchy has created a world in which nothing must get in the way of our ability to perform on demand. This mentality is both ableist and a disservice to the nature of our beings.

Even minor health issues like Samantha's can be challenging. Her given body is always fighting inflammation. Her food intake and hormones are intricately connected. Between the native stress of her body and the general stress of life, she is susceptible to becoming a blender of emotions, puffiness, irregular bleeding, and stomach aches. Medicine helps some; diet and an intentional focus on reducing external stress help the most.

Attending to the needs of her body remains a trial and error experiment. I contend that her very real physical symptoms are a reflection of the *pit in the stomach of humanity*. Aren't we all just trying to make it through a fucking day, being fucking human?

By trade Samantha is a communications wizard and branding guru. So, it's fitting that the greatest branding slogan of all time is a winning headline for her life.

Being Samantha makes me think of the Bissell, Inc. vacuum slogan: *Life's Messy. Clean It Up*. It brilliantly captures her essence. For real. Samantha vs. her teenage bedroom is a great analogy for our humanness.

While I am an organizational fiend, she was always more a *leave it where it lands* kind of person. When she was little, we would spend hours cleaning her room together, and a week later it was a disaster again. It got worse as she got older. Clothes strewn everywhere. If she knew I was around, I could hear her scampering to get everything off the floor shoved into her closet. I tried to have empathy for her teenage ways, but I simply couldn't understand how she could live in such chaos.

I tried a number of tactics, but nothing stuck. Finally, I sat her down and said I was out of tools. It was on her to learn how to master her surroundings. And off to college she went. When she was home for breaks, I didn't go there. If her room was a mess, I didn't comment or fix it. At least I tried not to. I always got busted.

Me: enters her room, hands clutched, jaw tight, aiming for nonchalant. "Hey!"

Samantha: "Hey!" Sees me eyeing the room. "I know, I know, but I was rushing. I've got this. Promise." *cue nervous laughter*

Me: picks something off the floor before reminding myself to put it down. "Okay!"

It was hard because clutter truly makes me anxious. My files are color coded, so is my closet, and my spices may just be alphabetized. By junior year I thought maybe her ability to keep things in order was getting a little better. And it was, for a minute, when life was calm and her boyfriend (now husband) was traveling abroad.

A bit of context. They met at Indiana University, day one, freshman year. They lived down the hall from each other in the Kelley Business School's "Living/Learning" dorm. She had chosen to study business at Craig's behest, and we'd joke that even if she didn't enjoy her classes, at least she'd meet some boys. The misogynistic jest wasn't funny, but in a seren-dipitous twist of fate, for her it proved to be true.

They had each other at *hello*. The attraction was magnetic, but felt forbidden. He is Christian and was raised to believe that Jewish folks are likely all going to hell. He could be *friendly* with Samantha, but not close friends, and certainly not lovers.

At school they were basically living together, but not transparently. His head, his heart, his loyalty, and his morality had him tied in knots. That proverbial *pit in the stomach* haunted him, too. Junior year offered him some reprieve through a semester abroad program in Spain. While he was there, they were able to communicate freely without him being filled with guilt about their relationship.

At the same time, her scholastic life changed drastically. She canceled her plans for an abroad program and opted instead to stay back and switch majors. It took courage to walk away from the prestigious business degree. Her departure was ironic, as she was one of the b-school's brand ambassadors. Her enthusiasm and zeal had placed her in a very visible position, but academically she was drowning.

Even after she transferred to the media school, the b-school wondered if she could stay on and represent them. They were only half kidding. It was clear that media was her bailiwick.

Her shift in majors highlights an important lesson. Sometimes the "right" path, the path that "makes sense," isn't actually right for us at all. Conversely, sometimes a misstep into the "wrong" path can be the "right" path because it provides some necessary soul learning.

All of these roads are part of the same video game of life lessons. The truth is, it's impossible to make a wrong turn; the key to success is to continue to hone your ability to tune into the steps that feel best for you at any given moment in time. Samantha's journey is case in point.

Once she tuned into herself, she was in a great spot. She felt loved, she was enjoying her studies, and she was able to snag a single room at her sorority. As the external chaos calmed, so did the internal chaos. But it was the calm before the storm.

Fast forward to her senior year, graduation weekend. By now she was taking 24 credit hours, repping a clothing brand, navigating what had become a tumultuous romantic relationship with future hubby, and looking for a job. On top of all that, she was recovering from a hideous case of strep throat that landed her in the ER from dehydration.

To add to the pressure, the weekend was also earmarked as the first time we would meet future hubby's parents. IU is in Bloomington, only a few hours away from Louisville. The plan was to come in for the day, go to her media graduation, future hubby's b-school graduation, say hi to his folks, grab a late lunch, then leave to head home. The town would be packed and it was unnecessary to fight the crowds for dinner and pay a pricey sum to stay at a Holiday Inn. The point was for them to celebrate with their friends and we lived close enough to let that happen.

Things didn't go according to plan. Future hubby made it to her graduation, but the fickle finger of fate took over. She was still feeling queasy from the strep and the ER had pumped her with tons of fluids which apparently were still in her system. She walked across the stage, shook the dean's hand, grabbed her diploma, smiled at the crowd, and kept on walking. Off the stage she went, before I saw her high tailing it in the direction of the restroom. I told future hubby and Craig to stay put and ran after her.

Yep, she tossed her cookies. We were there for an hour.

I popped out to assure future hubby and Craig that she was okay. I did believe this was just the fluids. I sent future hubby onward to his graduation. We would schedule another time to meet his folks.

She did in fact feel much better once she got the yucky out. We went to the drugstore, got some ginger ale and gluten free crackers. New plan. We'd drop her off, get her settled, and head home. She seemed like she would be fine, and hopefully she'd be able to participate in some of the weekend fun.

As we drove up to her house I could see the color coming back to her face.

Samantha: "Ya know what, I'm fine. What a classic story! Totally on brand! I'm actually relieved we didn't have to do the folks thing right now. I just need a nap and think I'll be able to celebrate tonight."

Me: "I agree, what a day! You definitely exited with a Big Bang! We are SO proud of you! I'm glad this chapter is behind you. We'll just come in for a minute."

Samantha: "Mom, you can't come into my house. My room is a mess. I can't deal with one more thing. Go home, I'm fine, really! I'll face my room after this weekend."

Me: "Don't be ridiculous. It can't be that bad. We'll fix it."

Well, it was. I pulled her into a huge hug. The mess was indicative of a problem way beyond a pile of discarded clothes. She was on the human hamster wheel of modernity, multitasking like her survival depended on it, and the state of her room reflected that life had spun her into a web of distress.

Wow, she was good at concealing her feelings. When I talked to her on the phone she was always upbeat. She was

Samantha. Her empathic nature meant she also tried to make herself available for me and everyone else, should we be having a problem. When I questioned her schedule, she said she had it under control. And she did, ish.

She was nailing her accomplishments and navigating the tenuous religious issues in her love life, but the enormous stress she was carrying manifested in the disaster of clothes, papers, pens, books, food wrappers, and hair ties that was her room. Things were piled so high I could barely walk through the door. It looked like a scene from HGTV's *Hot Mess House*.

Thinking she could, and should, do it all was preposterous. When I pointed this out to her, she broke down into a puddle of laughter and tears. I did too.

I sent Craig home and told him to come back and get me the next day. I stayed over and we pulled an all nighter talking about life, decluttering the mess and the tangle of emotions that had created it. Although she was feeling better, she was in no shape to go out. She could join her friends the next night, she needed to regroup. Future hubby was understanding and brought us some dinner.

I assured her there was no shame in feeling out of control. The mess was just an indication that things had gotten out of alignment for her. The experience was just another opportunity for growth. Facing it was the true graduation. By morning she could breathe and so could I. A tremendous weight had been lifted. The room looked great and so did she. Now she was free to truly enjoy the closure of this chapter and the immense soul learning it had provided.

So that's it? No generational trauma? Hell no. Samantha's

ADHD diagnosis provided insight into both the ableist divide and the general messiness of life. Having a name for it put her childhood difficulties into perspective, for both of us. All those times her room was a mess: she would sit there for hours unable to see how to navigate the clutter because of the way her brain worked. And then I would walk in with an eye roll. Ouch!

So much of her life has been spent overcompensating for the jumble in her brain. She's used her wits, her sarcasm, her charm, and her photographic memory to excel in a myriad of ways. Still, she always felt like she was either scrambling, being selfish, or underachieving. She felt like a fraud.

But as Samantha's story shows us, being human is messy!

Decluttering—emotionally, physically, and spiritually—was something that Samantha would always need to consciously add to her calendar and give priority to. She would have no choice in the matter. But neither do I, and neither do you.

In the coming chapters I'll share what this decluttering has looked like for me. Emotionally, I had to let go of what I thought was unconditional love. Physically, I had to reckon with my body and all the labels that have impeded my connection to my authentic self. Spiritually, I would have to find the pathway to my soul.

Generation WE simply can't keep shoving our shit under the rug and pretending it doesn't exist. Thus, I invite you to join me in my house cleaning. I'll share my vacuum. WE shift at the pace of ME. You next.

10
on parenting

To be clear, what you are reading is not a parenting manual. As in, a book on how to get better at raising kids. This is a book about creating better relationships with one another, regardless of the labels that bring us together. We also tend to think parenting is exclusive to the home front, but that is not the case. The home front is just the place we learn how to parent, from whatever our own caregiving situation looked like.

What I mean is, how we are parented is internalized, and it teaches us how to "parent" in the world.

Once in the world, we parent ourselves and each other all the time. For lack of better language, parenting is how we teach each other to get shit done. By this I mean that being parented literally taught us how to function: how to eat, how to stay clean, how to learn, how to work, and everything in between.

As noted, it is no coincidence that the structure of the familial grid and that of our political and religious institutions mirror one another. In the US, we are guided by the precepts of our "Founding Fathers." Likewise, a supreme being, or higher power, is often referred to as our Father, or Divine Parent. Putting the inherent sexism of this aside, you get the gist. Therefore, in order to create better, we need to revise how we parent one another across the board.

As it stands today, most of us have been parented didactically, myself included. The pain-triarchy has schooled us into believing there is a *right* and *wrong* way to be in the world. Stick with me because my point here is not about specific political or religious beliefs, it's about the binary in which we hold ourselves *regardless* of our beliefs on what is *proper* and *moral*.

The didactic parenting style upholds the status quo. In doing so, it encompasses the pain-triarchal hit parade of binaries: good/evil, right/wrong, pure/tainted. This is where we get into all the shoulds (and should nots) that have us out of balance with the nature of our humanness, which is dynamic, complex, and transitional.

But what if we could learn how to parent one another in a way that fully supported all of our authentic selves? This would enable us to parent interactively. In doing so, the intention would be to learn from each other and to cultivate collaboration free from expectations and judgments.

To be able to parent myself and my kids interactively, I would have to address the deep rooted pain-triarchy I had internalized from society and my primary familial grid. I had to question my adherence to the status quo. I had to question my own standards and guidelines. Did they bring me joy or pain? Did they inspire joy or cause pain in others? Was the voice that tells me *I'm on the right track* or that *I've fucked up* even valid?

Shifting from parenting didactically to interactively required the decluttering of my internal structure that I mentioned. It was like giving my chakras a *Marie Kondo* make-over. *Does this belief serve me or not? What about this emotion, this relationship, this attachment? What makes me feel scared? What makes me feel free? What can I make better? What do I need to let go? What would bring me joy, you joy, US joy?*

As I reviewed my relationships with both my mother and my kids, I was surprised by the culprit that kept us trapped in the didactic parent/child structure. It was the concept of *unconditional love*. Unconditional love, and its copilots, blind faith and devotion, had kept us from challenging the pain-triarchy, and thus, chained to the status quo. Unconditional love was impeding our shift from surviving to thriving. Hear me out.

Unconditional love suggests that either party gets to act however they want and still be loved. Sounds great, but it isn't. Unconditional implies that we should love without conditions. That's actually not true. We should love without expectations and judgments, which are very different from conditions. Boundaries are the conditions for a healthy relationship. Healthy relationships have healthy boundaries. Healthy boundaries include being accountable for one's actions.

Likewise, loving each other free from expectations and judgments is not an invitation for a free-for-all. On the contrary, the interactive parenting style requires each party to be an active participant in shared responsibility for the sustainability of the relationship. No one party pulls more weight; mutual respect is honored and mutual growth is fostered. I call this *untethered* love.

Here's an example of how unconditional love went awry between my mother and me. Whenever I tried to tell Roberta that she'd hurt my feelings, her response was that I should assume her actions were unintentional. But regardless of her intentions, for us to be in right relationship with each other, she needed to be accountable for the ways in which her actions impacted my feelings.

I can see why the concept of accountability was challenging for her. Accountability is a concept that exists outside the realm of the pain-triarchy, because accountability is not a judgment call; it speaks simply to a mutual consideration for the well-being of all involved.

Roberta couldn't handle my feelings, because she couldn't handle her own. She just pushed onward, never pausing to *Marie Kondo* her inner structure. She did not have the time, nor did she make the time, to address her baggage, and it was heavy. It was loaded with unresolved grief, anger, and disappointments. After a good amount of therapy, I realized the person carrying her bags was me.

With the early death of my grandfather, my mother's response was to do everything herself—because there really wasn't anyone else. She took the reins and found victory over a devastating situation. She remained a victor throughout her life, conquering every challenge that presented in her take-charge manner.

Arrogance was her survival mode because others had failed her greatly. In contrast, my survival mode was dependence. When I was confident of my point of view, I was self-assured. When I was afraid of her disapproval, I inadvertently offered to carry her bags, because I did not want to be another person who failed her. She, on the other hand, wanted to ensure that I was safe and cared for, and that manifested in controlling me.

Both my mother's arrogance and my dependence were the result of our generational trauma. I contend our reactions are not unique. In fact, I believe most of us are reeling between these two survival states: reliance on others (dependence) vs. self-reliance (arrogance). In one scenario, we are forced to rely on others due to circumstances, family hierarchy, laws, means, finances, etc. In the other scenario, others have failed us greatly and we feel we must rely solely on ourselves.

Potato, patato. Our reactions to challenges to our security are ultimately vested in that same fear: fear that we won't belong, fear that we won't be safe, fear that we will be abandoned. While my mother and I had opposite survival mechanisms, I would say my kids and I share dependence as our survival state. The mechanism doesn't matter, nor does it matter whether it's our physical safety, our emotional safety, or our ego that is compromised—when we feel threatened, we all go into survival mode.

And survival mode is inherently codependent. It's the unhealthy version of *we are in this together*.

It is important to note here that we *do* need each other to survive and, hopefully, to thrive. However, creating supportive, but independent, relationships is tricky. Caring for ourselves and each other is highly nuanced. It requires a dedication to honing our emotional intelligence. *And if historically our emotions have been sidelined as irrelevant to our survival, at this point in our evolution, they are critical.*

It is only as part of my awakening that I was able to shift

from a didactic parenting style to an interactive one. To become an interactive parent I had to loosen my grip on all of my attachments to perfectionism, acceptance, and conventions. In doing so, I had to loosen my grip on my attachment to belong to the world *outside myself* and instead practice belonging to *my inner self*. My favorite phrase has become: *said who*?

I no longer accept any information without questioning the source. Doing so empowers my confidence in myself, my thoughts, my feelings, my voice, and my intuition. You may be reading this and thinking, geez, why did she feel so disconnected from herself? Lemme say I used to think I was in a much more evolved state than I was. Abiding by the pain-triarchy gives one a false sense of security. Accessing our own truth is humbling and requires engaging our highest selves.

My codependency with my mother, the unconditional love between us, and her unyielding *perfectionism* for life is ultimately what set the stage for my deep investigation of what makes us humans tick. Beginning with what made the humans I am related to tick. Who was she to me? Who was I to my kids? What I discovered was that there were more similarities between us than I imagined, but also that our differences, although notable, did not obscure the core of our commonality. *The human desire to belong was at the center of all our beings.*

But remember: the pain-triarchy does not support belonging, it supports victory. Pulling my observations from myself into the world around me was this: whether the structure is our familial grid, our government, our religious affiliations, our places of employment etc., *belonging means conforming*. This is because these institutions are all built on didactic parenting models that are vested in survivalism.

Survivalism finds us molding each other to become copies of the pain-triarchy's version of humanity, not growing into the full spectrum of our unique humanness. And as with remaining blindly loyal to our parents, maintaining blind faith and devotion to systems that are broken also prevents us from evolving into more interactive paradigms.

Shifting from a didactic structure (surviving) to an interactive one (thriving) is a work-in-progress endeavor, so buckle up for the ride. WE didn't cause all the pain we are carrying, but WE must attempt to end the cycle. Doing so will take time, patience, accountability, and grace.

Generation WE comes prepared to do the work. Since we are evolving as a species, we are going to enter into each lifetime with a different skill set. This is good news! Interactive parenting pairs new skills with old in an effort to better meet the circumstances of the times we are living in. The process includes integrating intergenerational healing, knowledge, and wisdom.

11
trauma

When we embrace the idea of interactive parenting, each new generation presents an opportunity to evolve and heal the patterns inherent to the trauma we have accumulated with the history of the pain-triarchy. What is holding us back from living as authentic, complex, imperfect, loving beings is the labels, judgments, expectations, and fears that divide us. If we don't evolve, the trauma only becomes more deeply rooted and more difficult to extricate from our soul. It remains imprinted in our DNA.

I've shared some of my lay observations as to the day-to-day effects of generational trauma on my family. What I discovered was that I was circling around a concept with even broader implications that include both the meta-physical and the physical (as in scientific). Stick with me, it gets a little woo, but I think you'll find the connection between the two interesting.

Starting with the woo, I had a wild experience the day we dropped Chad off for his freshman year of college. I was never a helicopter parent, but the situation had propelled me into high gear protection mode. I wasn't concerned about Chad's ability to function on his own, nor did I need him attached to my hip. But I knew his queer story was ready to come out and I wanted him to be safe.

Safe physically and emotionally. Would his roommate be kind or an ass? Would it be a repeat of high school? Would he hide? Would he be able to be himself? *Was* he bi or gay? Did it matter? If he did only like men, would he be in danger of physical harm from homophobic hate crimes? The stories reported in the news, and shown in movies and books, were terrifying. My memories of the Pulse nightclub massacre will forever be etched into the pit of my stomach.

You get the gist. I was a mess. Of course I couldn't share this with Chad. I couldn't share it with Craig either. At this point in time, Chad's sexuality was implied between us, but Chad was not fully *out* to family or friends. For Chad's part, he was nervous, but excited.

His room was terrific. He was living in a residential college, as opposed to a dorm—a really cool concept that paired students with shared interests. This one was for creatives. The complex was divided into quads, with two students per unit, each with their own room, connected to a bathroom shared by eight kids. Community and space, that was good. His roommate seemed nice. We kissed goodbye.

Afterwards, Craig and I grabbed dinner and drinks at a restaurant near campus. While I couldn't vent my full on angst, we shared in the bittersweet moment of this transition. Samantha was in her senior year of college; we were now officially "empty-nesters." The wine calmed my nerves a bit. By the time we finished our meal, I was exhausted and ready to call it a night.

But Craig wanted to grab a nightcap at the hotel bar with all the other parents. He struck up a conversation with a nutritionist. They talked for over an hour. He was fascinated by her innovative and holistic theories on food and health. I chimed in at the beginning before turning to chat with the folks seated nearest to me. I immediately picked up on the fact that the nutritionist was a seeker. I could tell she knew I was too.

Shit! I was in no mood to play the energy game. I didn't want to talk about the beyond. I wanted to go to bed. But by the time the bar closed, she and Craig were still talking. We moved to a small lounge area. Before I even sat down on the oversized leather sofa, she called me out: *Was I aware of my energetic gifts*? I was still in the early stages of my awakening, and my response was, *I think so* ...

Within moments, the Holocaust came up. I don't remember how. She went on to share that the trauma from that atrocity was part of my soul DNA. At the time I had no idea that generational trauma was even a thing, I just knew that she was onto something; the Holocaust kept coming up for me in both my daily life and in my therapy sessions with my energetic healer.

The nutritionist wanted me to know that my purpose involved the healing of generational trauma, mine and others. She told me that I had a natural ability to communicate wisdom and that my voice would help folks shift out of pain into joy by activating their sixth sense.

WTF! Now I was awake and intrigued.

Craig, the non-believer, was ashen as he watched on. At least I had a witness. It felt like we were in an episode of the

Twilight Zone. She could tell I was shook, but she assured me that our encounter would unlock something critical in me. The electricity coursing through my body was super charged. When we said goodnight, she gave me a bear hug and wished me well in my next steps.

The serendipity was overwhelming. During the previous year I had been writing extensively about the sixth sense. It started as a blog, that morphed into a draft of a book, that would eventually become this book. Over the summer, while Chad was taking a break before college, he'd offered to help me with the finishing touches. We were natural collaborators, as we both were trying to lasso in the intersecting concepts of self-discovery and social justice.

My encounter with the nutritionist felt like a sign from the universe, confirmation that Chad and I were both exactly where we needed to be. Apparently the University of Virginia was part of the plan. For me, that moment solidified my path. Six years and thousands of words later, here we are.

So, how does the meta-physical aspect of generational trauma impact me, and in turn you?

Let's begin with the nutritionist's observation about the Holocaust. While this travesty did not only affect Jewish people, they were the main target of Hitler's genocidal campaign. Thus, as a Jewish person I am zero degrees of separation from the fear that it could happen again. I am also one degree of separation from the incident itself; my dad was a World War II vet.

From my soul history to my lived reality, being Jewish has meant being *other*. In this otherness, I was an outcast before my first breath. In this otherness, my belonging is inherently challenged. In this otherness, my safety is always in question. In this otherness, my perfectionism runs rampant because I want, *need*, to fit in. In this otherness, superiority has me flailing, wondering how to uphold the status quo while hoping that I don't wind up at the bottom of the heap.

In this otherness, my life is a house of cards resting precariously on the concepts of acceptance and rejection. Acceptance and rejection are the pillars of the double bind created by the pain-triarchy. I meet acceptance from those who are *like me*, formulating community. I meet rejection from those who *fear me* because I am not like them. Including my own kin when I fail to conform.

Besides being Jewish, I have also felt *other* in my gender. I have felt unseen. Chad has felt *other* in his orientation. He has felt immoral. Samantha has felt *other* in her neurodivergence. She has felt like an imposter.

So, I ask you, if we are the *other*, who exactly is the *in-group*? Are you? Are you superior to us? Why? Is it your skin color? Your religion? Your gender? Your orientation? Your brains? Your abilities? What makes you *in* and us *out*?

The belief that superiority equals better is the root of our generational trauma.

Despite all the ways that we feel inferior, most of us appear fine on the outside. But I contend we are not. Add *otherness* to the daily trauma of being human—natural disasters, the extortionate cost of healthcare, mental unwellness, accidents, broken hearts, career pressures, economic instability, etc.—and the ongoing threat to our safety can feel like a tangled web of never-ending fear. Fear we often don't even realize we are carrying because living with it has become the norm.

Again, from paper cuts to severed limbs, we all share a history of being hurt, being *othered*, and we have all been imprinted with the binary limitations of survivalism. Biologically, when we don't reckon with the root of the fear that caused the trauma in the first place, we literally pay the trauma imprints of the past forward. The damage is psychological, physical, and apparently epigenetic.

Which is where the science catches up with the woo.

Dr. Rachel Yehuda, a professor of trauma-related psychiatry and neuroscience, is currently conducting studies showcasing how "adverse experiences can change future generations through epigenetic pathways."

Included in her research are survivors of the Holocaust. She has discovered that both the survivors *and* their descendants carried unusual levels of cortisol in their systems, resulting from the indescribable horrors they witnessed and experienced. Whether notably high or low, the unusual levels of cortisol appear to have been genetically passed on to their children *and* their grandchildren, resulting in increases of conditions like asthma and anxiety disorders.

The post-traumatic stress disorder (PTSD) experienced by one generation gets passed on to another by both genetics and storytelling. In regard to the Holocaust, we intentionally relive the atrocity in museums, books, plays, poems, podcasts, etc. We expose ourselves, our children, and others to the story in graphic detail with hopes that this will prevent it from happening again.

The side effect of this is that it is not uncommon for Jewish folks, whether direct descendants of the Holocaust or not, to live in daily fear of this atrocity. The persecution of one's people is a terrifying thing to identify with, especially as a child. Today, this fear intersects with an intense pressure to recapture what was sacrificed. *They died so I must live, I must procreate, I must achieve, I must be happy.*

And antisemitism is flourishing, with some folks even denying that the Holocaust even happened. Between the ongoing threat to our survival and the survivor's guilt carried over from the past, the trauma loop continues.

Now let's multiply this by all the other versions of generational trauma. Colonialism. Slavery. Homophobia. Misogyny. The pain of a parent telling you that you are stupid and society telling you that your body is all wrong.

Ultimately, generational trauma is vested in the inter-generational pains caused by survivalism, which in turn is caused by greed. The greed of those in power has us trapped in a scarcity mindset, whereby only some of us are deemed worthy of having our needs met. What follows? Fear that we won't make the cut, or the literal experience of persecution, poverty, and oppression.

We've been through a LOT as a species, so it makes sense that we are carrying a lot. But we do ourselves and each other a massive favor when we find a way to divest from tragedy and break the patterns of the past. We can do this by embracing our internal evolutions, and tuning in to our Higher Self. In doing so, we begin to heal our souls.

Breaking past patterns requires going through your baggage and digging deep through its contents. Yes, it is a laborious task, but one we can't avoid if we want to continue to evolve. Embarking on this process is how we can bridge our stories and work together to create a world in which we all feel like we belong.

WE have the opportunity to transition from receiving an inherited past to participating interactively with our history to create a future worth passing on.

12
chosen family

To become me, I need to feel at home in my skin and in my surroundings. Easier said than done! I'm telling you: the pain-triarchy is a homewrecker.

This is because pain-triarchy is a fear based paradigm. As I have mentioned, its fundamental structure, the familial grid, is the petri dish for all judgments and expectations. This is where divides around gender, class, race, orientation, religion, ability, and size are seeded, as sewn by the survivalist aspects of our heritage.

The pain-triarchal familial grid is also where the failure of the Golden Rule begins and ends.

*Treat others as you would **like to be treated.***

Not

*Treat others **as you have been treated** (which has likely been horrible).*

Or

*Treat others **as you treat yourself** (which, sadly, has also not been great, given that most of us feel like we are not worthy of great treatment).*

In requiring us to conform, the pain-triarchal values do not breed compassion or authenticity. Fit in the box or you are out. Extreme examples of this are conversion therapy, or being excommunicated for marrying outside of your religion. And then there is the everyday pain we often endure at home. Bad grade, you're an idiot; missed the shot, you're a failure. Whether the result of big T or little t traumas, the suffering is real.

My pain in this lifetime is deeply tied to that of the LBGTQ+ community. How we treat folks who identify as queer not only hits close to home, but serves as a great representation of just how shitty human beings can be to one another in general.

For the big Ts, stories like Alan Turing's reverberate through my body. He was the Brit responsible for breaking Nazi codes. Had he been straight, he'd have been a hero. But he was gay, and despite his talents and service to his country, his own people convicted him of gross indecency and chemically castrated him, pushing him ultimately to commit suicide.

As for the little t's, we have situations where folks just make really stupid comments. Like a friend who recently commented to *me* about a man who got married in his forties, "his family was so relieved—at least he's not gay." No physical harm, just a very deep paper cut. I called them out and we moved on, but this kind of casual bigotry is hurtful and exhausting.

As a society, we tend to treat anybody who doesn't fit into the pain-triarchal "norm" like shit. Sometimes, if they express talents that are useful to the hierarchical power structures, they are placed on a pedestal, before being subject to being tortured, maimed, killed, ostracized, rejected, and ridiculed simply because of who they *love* or how they *identify*.

In response to this hideous treatment, often at the hands

of their own biological kin, the queer community created the concept of chosen family. I was searching for the best way to explain the concept and discovered this wonderful quote from social scientist, Dr. Bahiyyah Maroon: "A chosen family is made up of people who have intentionally chosen to embrace, nurture, love, and support each other regardless of blood or marriage."

Within Generation WE, regardless of how we identify or what big Ts and little t's we carry, we are all tasked with choosing how we want our families to be. Our families may be biological, adopted, or found; but they are never a "given." Regardless of blood, we need to work hard at our family relationships for them to be successful. We need to demonstrate that it's okay to trust one another. We do this by being vulnerable with each other. By showing support for one another. By growing with one another.

Sure, I always had a close relationship with my kids. I had a close relationship with my mother too. But close isn't chosen. To varying degrees, "close" included the conditions of the pain-triarchy and the fear from the expectations and judgments it brings with it. The COVID-19 lockdown was instrumental in transitioning us from a "given" family dynamic to a *chosen* one.

When the pandemic struck, Chad was home on spring break and he just stayed. A few months later, when Samantha's Chicago lease was up, she and her now husband moved in with us too. Their jobs, his college graduation, internships, and grad school applications were all remote. We are incredibly fortunate to have a big house, with plenty of space to accommodate everyone very comfortably. The basement and spare bedrooms doubled as offices, providing each person with a place to sleep and work. We live near a grocery store, so access to food was easy too. Dinner was usually eaten together, spent watching episodes of *Top Chef* and *The Great British Bake-off*, comfort-food shows that gave us a breather from the troubles of the world.

Five adults under one roof, with my mother around the corner, and our family therapist on speed dial. And so it was that the worst of times provided the best possible opportunity for choosing one another fully.

I was a few years into my awakening at the time, and now the unusual circumstances brought me face-to-face with the roots of my deepest wounds.

My mother's health was taking a rapid decline. By the start of 2020, her lungs and heart were beginning to go south. Things came to a head April 1, 2020. It wasn't a funny April Fools. She was feeling spry and tripped doing a breathing test at the pulmonologist's office. The fall left her in a wheelchair requiring fulltime assistance. Even with help from in-home caregivers, tending to my mother became a fulltime job for me. Her emotional and physical well-being were my utmost concern.

For her, the isolation of the pandemic was understandably crushing. She couldn't get out. My siblings and her other grandchildren couldn't visit. We made the best of it, but it was taxing for everyone involved, especially Roberta and me. She alternated between verbally abusing me for caring for her ... and praising me for caring for her. The passive/aggressive element of our relationship was at an all-time high and it had me cracking at the seams. It was awful. I am beyond grateful my grown kids were with me. They held me while I held her. They helped hold her too. Then I held them while they faced some of their demons regarding work and interpersonal growth.

Emotions that had been simmering below the surface were coming to a boil for each of us. For me, my values, my morality, and my soul itself were being challenged, both by events in the external world and at home. My vision had been sharpened by my awakening and the view was intense.

The deaths of George Floyd and Breonna Taylor high-lighted the extent to which Black lives *did not* matter. The rise of antisemitism was overwhelming. Trump's response to both the pandemic and the violence was terrifying. My mother's approval of Trump made it worse. She watched Fox News all day long. I tried to side step any discussion about world events with her, but it was tough.

By December of 2020, I was at a tipping point. My mother was too. I took her to lunch at one of our favorite spots. Since we couldn't go in, we had a car picnic in the parking lot. We did stuff like this daily. We were having a good time, chatting and being silly. Then something came up about her financial af-fairs, and she lost it. She started screaming and swearing at me. When she gained her composure, she tried to apologize. But I simply couldn't, and wouldn't, take it anymore. It didn't matter that she was dying. No situation called for this type of behavior.

My hand had been forced. I could let things stay as they were, or I could stand up for what was right for *me*. I kept my cool and got her to her home. Luckily, her favorite aide was on duty. She had witnessed some of this behavior between Rob-erta and me before and I knew she was a safe space. I told her what was up and said I'd be back once I'd had time to digest my feelings.

I took a time-out and wrote a letter to my mom. I knew real growth beyond the pain-triarchy would not be possible for us, but that in the meantime I could follow the Golden Rule, stay in my power, and still choose to show her love. It was my chance to be an interactive parent to myself. It was my chance to set a healthy boundary for ME.

That evening I made a plan. I would read my mother my letter, with the aide as my witness. I was so nervous! My mother was glad to see me. She was sitting in her chair, look- ing fresh from the good care of the aide. She tried to be chipper and side step what had happened earlier. No dice. I clutched my letter and told her things were not okay between us. I told her she had to listen to me, that I had prepared a letter so as not to have my thoughts derailed. She was not permitted to respond until I was done. She was respectful as my quivering voice recited my words.

To paraphrase: I let her know I understood that she was in a dreadful place, but that this didn't entitle her to treat me like crap. I told her that if she said anything shitty to me again, I would not respond; I would simply leave. I reminded her that she was in good hands with all of her caregivers. I promised to come back once I had cooled off, but that never again would she speak to me with disrespect. That was it. I wasn't mean, I didn't try to explain things. I simply stated how I would be handling my energy moving forward.

She was both shocked and apologetic. I was kind, but in- different. We had been here before, but never on my terms. In this moment, I was redefining the terms of our relationship and inviting her to become part of my *chosen* family. I was asking her to see and accept all of me, not just the version that it suited her to see. I don't know what my letter did for her, but for me the encounter was illuminating. I'd wanted for so long to believe that our power dynamics were *her* problem. But now I realized this was not the case. *Giving me my power had never been her responsibility; it was all mine.*

In this reckoning with my mother, a light was cast on my relations with everyone else. About a week later, I tripped over Samantha. It was a Friday. Chad was going to a friend's, but she and her now hubby said they wanted to do a Shabbat dinner. So I went to the store and got all the fixings. As I was getting things prepared, she informed me of a change in plans. Future hubby had had a really bad day at work, so they were going to do their own thing. This usually wouldn't bother me, but I was exhausted and pissed! Again, I felt taken for granted.

I lost it. I told everyone I needed space and was going to spend the night at a friend's. I had never done anything like this before. They were as stunned as me. I did go to my friend's, but I came home after I calmed down. It was nearly midnight. The next day Chad invited me to go on a drive with him. He asked what happened and told me I was unduly harsh with Samantha. I knew he was right, but something between all of us was off. I realized I had positioned myself as everyone's conveyor belt. I was the one carrying all the bags.

But just like with my mother, *giving me my power was not their responsibility; it was all mine*. I wrote another letter to my family and delivered it that night. This one I didn't read, I

117

handed them each a copy.

Bottom line, I made it clear that my authentic self was ready to make her debut and that I would be accepting nothing less of anyone else. No more dancing around our issues. If I felt dismissed or hurt, I was going to say so, and they needed to as well. My husband and I were not always on the same page politically; that too was no longer up for discussion. I was me and he had to be him. I would no longer be making myself smaller for my mother, my husband, or anyone else.

It was a long night of conversations. The kids and Craig, the kids and me, the kids and each other, me and Craig. I didn't have all the answers, I told them, but I sure had a lot of questions. In the meantime, I needed a verbal commitment from them. Were we choosing each other? Did we unequivocally agree to grow together and to support one another in this growth, without allowing fear and judgment and perfectionism to wedge themselves between us?

Becoming each other's chosen ones meant everyone had to be welcomed into the relationship as they were, and wherever they were at in terms of their evolution. In this moment, Samantha, Chad, and I shifted more fully into an interactive parenting dynamic. Even Craig was trying to get the hang of it, which was helpful. Most importantly, in choosing each other, we stopped taking one another for granted.

Including me. I could no longer take myself for granted. I heard the cabin crew in my head, "put your own mask on first." Breathing 101. If I couldn't breathe, how useful was I going to be to anybody?

If my given family was also going to be my chosen family,

then I would also have to choose me. To choose me, I would need to enact the full meaning of the Golden Rule.

*Treat others as you would **like to be treated**.*

I was a quick study when it came to how I treat others. I had plenty of desire to do right by my fellow humans. Whenever I was off in a transaction, I became ready and willing to rectify the situation. What proved to be more difficult was learning to treat myself with the same respect, empathy, and love that I offered others.

I could understand that *you* were enough, were worthy of being treated with understanding, respect, and dignity, but somehow *I* still felt undeserving. This seems to be a common theme among us. So many of us feel like we are not enough. Why is this?

13
enough

In a word, again, victory. Survivalism makes it very clear: we are not all equal. Again, for those in the back: for me to win, you must lose. Therefore, only some of us are worthy of life, love, and the pursuit of happiness. Survivalism had lied to me and in doing so, severed me from my authentic self.

To meet the real me, I would need to evict the pain-triar-chal voice in my head that told me I was *fat, ugly, stupid, and lazy*. Four little words that I had used to trash my body and my brain on the daily. Four little words that held the venom of my oppression. What are yours?

For me, *fat-ugly-stupid-lazy* was my response to feeling like I didn't belong. It would catch me off guard and take me unex-pectedly down a rabbit hole of despair.

A critical moment occurred my freshman year of high school. A senior asked me to prom. We quickly fell in step with each other. It was that first love, filled with vulnerability, sincerity, and naïveté. He saw all of me and encouraged me to occupy that space. The feeling was reciprocal. We felt like we *belonged* together and we both flourished in the relationship.

We shared a wonderful summer.

Fall came and he left for college. We both knew things would likely fizzle, but our connection had been stabilizing for both of us. We agreed to see how things played out. And then my mom broke us up, right before winter break, right before his finals. As I mentioned, she had married young and didn't want me to fall into the same rut.

She had a notion of what an *ideal* life would look like for me, and sticking with my high school sweetheart wasn't it. I wasn't in harm's way, we both knew that. But she was clear; she wanted to protect me from the hurts she had sustained, from the struggles and disappointments she had encountered.

She truly believed she was doing right by me, but what happened was the transference of her trauma to me. Every arena where she had felt *not enough* was a place she wanted victory for me. She wanted a seat at the table, to climb up a rung up on the ladder of hierarchy, affluence, and power. I didn't begrudge her these things, I wanted them too. So I agreed; breaking up with him was in my best interest.

Was it? In retrospect, I truly believe things would have ended naturally over time. But had I been able to stay in the relationship a little longer, like, until I was ready to leave it, would my self worth have been a bit more stable? Or, as she feared, would I have become *less* of myself?

What transpired was the advent of an eating disorder. This wasn't the result of the breakup, per se, it was the concept of striving for the *ideal life* that had me lost. What was it, and what would be required of me to get there? My mother seemed to have it all figured out for me, and I desperately wanted her approval. So I tried to follow her lead, as I flirted with a case of binge eating disorder. I also began smoking.

My appearance, my intelligence, and my productivity had felt *not good enough* from as early as I could remember. This was not my mother's fault. No amount of praise or approval I received from her could counteract the broader pain-triarchal programing I internalized about my worth and what it looked like.

If I could just be thinner, prettier, smarter, and faster, surely *then* I would be worthy of an *ideal life*. Basically, if I could only *not be me*. Well, that certainly left lots of runway for *fat-ugly-stupid-lazy* to kick me in the ass. It didn't matter who I loved, who loved me, how thin I was, or what accolades I received. The feeling of being *not enough* continued to haunt me.

Take a minute to pause here and reflect on your own story. What's your version of *fat-ugly-stupid-lazy*? What sucker punch did the pain-triarchy deliver via a parent, a teacher, a friend, or a societal expectation that still makes you feel like shit? Who first told you you were ugly? What test did you fail? What assignment got turned in late? What game did you blow? What achievement missed the mark?

My point here is not to cast blame, nor do I believe life should be all smooth sailing. My point is that we are all in the same jam. I learned that my lack of internal worth wasn't personal, it was universal. The pain-triarchal values of idealism and perfectionism hold each of us to standards that are impossible to obtain (let alone maintain). Standards, in and of themselves, that are rooted in the binary; this is *good*, that is *bad*.

Standards are the mile markers of victory. They keep us trapped in a precarious game of comparison. Belonging is the prize, and our worth is the currency. Of course the standards are arbitrary and subjective, they can't be anything else. Yet, we all keep playing along as if *someday* we will crack the code and win the affirmation we crave. What a crock!

Thanks to the pursuit of victory we are trapped in a cycle of *not enough* that is based on harmful, inaccurate, and archaic beliefs.

Did you know that adolescent and young females are disproportionately represented in eating disorders? Did you know that the balding complex has its roots in the Freudian argument that male hair is symbolic to male genitals, thus equating hair loss with castration? Did you know that eugenics created myths regarding intelligence as being a factor of race? Did you know that laziness is a puritanical myth based on the "sin" of idleness that has been used to prop up slavery and capitalist gain?

A critical part of enacting Generation WE is to stop questioning our worth.

I was astounded to learn a simple fact: self-abuse is also an abuse of power. It never occurred to me that the voice in my head that told me I was *fat, ugly, stupid, and lazy* was just as hurtful as if those words were being hurled at me by someone else. In fact, I realized I'd often hurl them before someone else had the chance.

This counterintuitive form of self-protection is another triumph for the pain-triarchy. It keeps the pain-triarchy in business. Who amongst us can claim they have never berated themselves in this way?

It hurts to know that after all the trauma we've endured, WE, in fact, are responsible for our own rescue. To see that our pain has clouded our vision. That survivalism has us lost in the thick of the forest. Abuse of power is what keeps us from thriving, self-abuse included.

Thus, I have decided I am simply no longer allowed to trash talk myself. Period. I stop my kids in their tracks when I hear them doing it too. It is NOT okay. That negative talk is our internal pain-triarchy. And it's bullshit.

Now, every time I want to beat myself up for saying the wrong thing, misunderstanding something, eating too much, oversleeping, being late, tired, cranky, sensitive, or sad, I internally flag my behavior. Then, I literally force myself to rephrase the thought as I would say it to someone else.

Me to you: "You are running late, NP! It happens. I'm the queen of late. Just get here safely. If you need to, we can reschedule. No worries!"

Old me to myself: "You are such a fucking idiot! You always think you can get more done than you can. You are so inefficient. You wasted their time and deserve their wrath."

New me to myself: "Time can be tricky for you, so cut yourself some slack. Your brain and body do not work as fast as you think they do. Try to schedule things better, and keep practicing your relationship to your process. Practice to improve, not to be perfect. You've got this!"

Which voice sounds most like yours? The trash talker or the supportive voice that always strives to offer constructive guidance?

To truly create better, together, we must learn to see ourselves as the content creators of our future. To see our inherent (versus inherited) value as given. This is a drastic departure from our current reality. To believe we are enough, we must excavate the history of *fat-ugly-stupid-lazy*, and replace it with a foundation that supports *all* of our humanness.

14
heritage

Bring on the bulldozers.

If the pain-triarchy is a homewrecker, religion is the builder responsible for the damage. I am not saying religion is inherently awful, I'm saying it has been abused by the pain-triarchy. To the extent that I believe religion is the culprit for our universal feeling of unworthiness.

Religion was created as a tool to manage the vast domain of our humanness and to help us interpret the majesty of nature. It told our common stories, informed our understanding of the psychological and biological aspects of being human, and offered guardrails for how to live together.

Ultimately, religion helped bring order to the chaos of the universal forces swirling within and around us. At a time when our humanity was still nascent, our survival became dependent on it. However, as we gained a greater understanding of the functions of both our bodies and nature, we began to establish another tool for trying to make sense of the human condition: science.

Spirit and *science*.

Where did one end and the other begin? That was, indeed, the question. Personally, I believe the two are fundamentally intertwined. Investigating the complicated relationship between spirit and science is another topic entirely. For our purposes here, I'm going to focus on the tenuous relationship between religion and spirituality.

In the guise of religion, spirituality has come to mean rules, moral codes, and acceptable means of behavior. It has been boiled down to "good vs. evil." Its legacy forms the basis for our concepts of family, society, and country.

We are a group of people, these are our rules, this is how we live.

I'd like to think religion set out to create justice, to make things fair, and to honor our inherent needs as a species. But it has become corrupted and used as a weapon to be aimed against one another, even within our own families. So many religious tenets teach misogyny, bigotry, homophobia, and xenophobia. That is not spirituality. Spirituality is about honoring the light that illuminates our humanity: both individually and as part of a universal ecosystem.

If religion was about spirituality, we wouldn't be in this mess. We would be living in a world that honored the dignity and well-being of everyone, and neither you nor I would feel so crappy about ourselves or so scared of one another.

Look at all the ways religious systems have failed us. The hypocrisy is overwhelming. People lie, cheat, and kill—as if these acts being conducted "in the Lord's name" justifies everything. There is no room for wisdom or nuance in our current religious worldview; we have created an environment where we use the name of the "Lord" to promote survivalism.

Sometimes this is done out of malice, sometimes out of fear, and sometimes from naïveté.

It really doesn't matter. Religion has caused enormous pain, not unity. The current subjugation of women's rights regarding body autonomy in the US, and the lack of choice regarding the wearing of religious clothing in India and Iran, are but a few examples of the millions of ways religion is used as a weapon of mass destruction. Women make up half of the world's population. How is this still our reality? At what point will we get that the inhumane treatment of some affects *us all*?

Equality hurts no one, and yet, we have been taught that we can't all have it all.

Said who?

We need to separate religion as in doctrine, from religion as a doorway to a spiritual path, from religion as a cultural identity. Religion as a doctrine is vested in binary values. Religion as a doorway to a spiritual path explores freely the texts of a faith and utilizes them as a pathway to our universal connectivity. Religion as a cultural identity represents the lifestyle, folklore, and ethnic belonging shared by a specific group of people.

When considering our relationship with religion we must ask ourselves: exactly what doctrine are we following, and why? What got said by whom, and when? Do the rules, the values, the ethics, and the moral codes still fit? Does the treatment of others as defined by "right" or "wrong" still make sense? Is it morality at the mic, or is it coercion?

Throughout the ages, lots of people have also said some very wise things *in the name of the Lord*. But wisdom is not stagnant.

Sometimes those same folks have also done some very shitty things, which might not have seemed so shitty in the context of the times. Now that we have the power of hindsight, it is on us to detangle the wisdom from the dogma, and to take only what serves us forward.

I searched for a word that could best represent a break from the binary doctrines of religion and speak more to the spirit and culture piece. *Heritage* is what kept surfacing, so let's talk about it.

Typically heritage is thought of as something inherited: the observance of rituals passed down through the ages, ensuring our connection with our ancestors. What if *inherited* became *integral*? What if an amalgamation of the past, present, and future was what is actually necessary for our *heritage* to remain a relevant part of our humanity.

In Hebrew, we have a saying. *L' dor v dor*. It has been interpreted to mean *from generation to generation*.

The implication is that we are *obligated* to pass along our religion, our country, our culture, our ideals, our morality, and our love, from one generation to another in the name of something greater than us (aka God).

This phrase has always been quite special for me. It connected me to my ancestors and made me feel like part of something bigger than myself. However, another one of the tenets of Judaism is the responsibility to challenge what is. And so, I challenge *L' dor v dor*. I think we should change the preposition *to* to *with*, switch *obligation* to *opportunity*, and shift the focus from outside ourselves, to within ourselves.

Generation with generation, we have the opportunity to pass along what works and leave behind what doesn't, in the name of something great within us.

This shift in text speaks to the concept of Generation WE. It is on us, Generation WE, to reclaim our spiritual and cultural *heritage* and create a legacy that blends tradition with modernity. In doing so, we can activate the integration of all that unites us, instead of focusing on what divides us.

My family got to experience this shift first hand with Samantha and her husband's wedding. Their union was a stunning example of generational healing. As I mentioned, their relationship was fraught with obstacles due to their religious differences.

On my part, I was supportive of whatever her heart told her was her truth. Things between them had begun to heat up just as my awakening was beginning to unfold; my whole-hearted support was a huge departure from younger me. As I have stated, marrying within my faith was a serious issue for my family and a choice I had made for myself, twice.

I enjoyed sharing my Judaism with both X and Craig. It was an enormous part of my identity. It still is, but from a much freer perspective. What's important to note here is that I had to be able to separate my identity from Samantha's. That sounds easy, but I want to pause and allow this to sink in.

Separating ourselves from all of the mores of the pain-triarchy isn't easy at all. When Samantha first mentioned that she sometimes attended church with her now hubby and enjoyed some of the teachings, it felt like an affront: to me, to her upbringing, to our family, to our community, to our religion.

Due to my budding awakening, I knew not to react to those feelings. I let them digest, because I was aware that my feelings were just a byproduct of my own evolution. Just as I was learning that my own identity could not be contained by labels and binary thought patterns, the same was true for her. This was her story, not mine. She wasn't rejecting me, she was finding herself. She wasn't abandoning anything, she was exploring everything to see what was right for her.

I cannot highlight this strongly enough. We must separate the ME in the WE for the dynamic of Generation WE to work. Each of us is on our own spiritual, intellectual, emotional, and physical journey. We grow into WE when we assist each other in becoming authentically ME.

In any event, navigating their growing love for each other was a turbulent ride. His folks emphatically did not approve of the situation. At first he tried to hide their relationship from them. Once he was brave enough to share a little, he was met with their full-on rejection. I understood.

I had experienced this in my own family over thirty years ago. My younger brother's wife wasn't Jewish. My folks tipped dangerously close to *kriah*, which refers to the act of tearing one's clothes to indicate Jewish mourning. Yes, as in "you are dead to the family."

To some of you this may sound unbelievable, so I'll spell it out. Marrying outside our faith was a flat NO. The allegiance to faith, family, history, our country, and Israel was a mixed bag of obligation, tradition, responsibility, culture, and joy. My folks were concerned that my brother was abandoning the fibers of his being for what might be a fleeting romance.

They really pressed him. It was offered as a binary choice. Was he going to choose love over everything else? Would he be happy with his choice? How would they raise their children? Would she convert to Judaism? Would he change religions?

My folks refused to meet my sister-in-law until he firmly chose love. In their defense, they claimed all along that if he liked her, they knew they would too. It wasn't about her *person*, or his; to them it was about something bigger. But if he went ahead and chose love, this they could understand, especially my mother. Remember, she didn't necessarily believe in God, she believed in tradition and, in turn, conviction. My dad probably had more of an attachment to the religious part. Between them, their views were sincere but complicated, and fraught with loopholes and either/ors.

Once my brother announced his engagement, love was honored, and the two of them were left to create whatever world suited them. Their union was celebrated in joy. All I remember from the day itself was my enormous relief that I wasn't going to lose my brother!

Yes, the trauma of the previous years just melted away. We were all exhausted and glad that peace had been restored to our family. At the end of the day, my brother and his wife did opt to raise their family in the Jewish faith, but this was their choice too. Witnessing them figure things out, with love at the forefront of their story, set into motion a good amount of evolution for my family as a result.

By the time the next generation, my kids and their cousins, started marrying, keeping it *in-the-faith* was no longer a requirement. I'm well aware that such a shift isn't necessarily ground breaking: most of my friends have interfaith marriages. The point is that we shifted. For my family, an enormous part of our generational trauma was on the way to being healed.

However, the moral crisis in the relationship between Samantha and her husband was even more extreme, with no resolution presenting itself. Some days his folks seemed to be on board, other days not at all.

After college, he and Samantha moved to Chicago. Within a few years, they moved in together, this time transparently. When the pandemic hit they moved to Louisville and, as I mentioned, lived with us while working remotely. Meanwhile, Samantha continued to try and gain his family's acceptance. We did too. Our meetings were always cordial.

Unfortunately, while his folks were *nice* to her face, ours too, their angst over religion proved their actions to be disingenuous. Please know this was not their intention. I wholeheartedly believe they wanted to relate. Becoming each other's *relations* was more challenging.

Emotions were high. I held the fragile couple tightly and made most of the plans, leaving them to focus on how to approach his folks. They tried candor, love, and letters. In return, his parents made it clear that they would attend the wedding, but that they disapproved.

His folks feared that him marrying a non-Christian, and someone Jewish at that, might literally wind him up in *hell*. I know nothing about this concept, but I do know it was real for them. It was what they had been taught. It was part of *their* generational trauma.

The level of pain this belief caused hurt my soul. It's hard for me to imagine anything worse than the pain we cause each other, is *that* not hell? And the blatant disregard for my daughter and their son? I knew this hurt them too. The loss all around was devastating. I heard a phrase in my head offering guidance: *be gentle with those who are the harshest.* Gentle is not the same as compliant. Gentle offers grace and creates space for growth.

With grace leading the way, I helped Samantha and hubby let go of the expectation that their wedding would be the best day of their life. They had already experienced many wonderful days together, and there would be many more to come. This would likely be their *bravest* day.

In the end, they chose not to elope. Not COVID-19, not a venue change, not family interference: nothing was going to prevent them from making a public declaration of their love. They chose our family therapist to officiate—and the resulting interfaith wedding replaced obligation with exploration, and tradition with ritual. In doing so, the newlyweds created for themselves the opportunity to *thrive*, because they chose to honor their connection to spirituality, and each other, from a place of freedom, not fear.

One doesn't need to experience an interfaith union to heal our generational trauma with religion. WE just have to embrace our spiritual and cultural heritages in ways that bring us joy without the judgment or pressure for it to always look a certain way.

For me, my current connection to my religion is a bit more like my sober curious journey: it's not an all or nothing ordeal. I'm particularly interested in the universal teachings of mysticism, and in spiritual beliefs that connect body, mind, and soul. I'm curious about rituals. How does a ritual you embrace connect you to source? What rituals connect me? What places, spaces, and thoughts bring you into community? Into yourself? What works for me? For you? For WE?

We don't need to throw away religion; a shift into heritage allows our concepts of religion to evolve as WE do. As it stands, we are relying on archaic texts to guide us into the future. A practice which is not only counterintuitive, but also vested in harmful binary codes of morality and conduct. Generation WE must question the roots of our religious worldviews and challenge their impact, personally and collectively. WE can't grow if we are unwilling to investigate the foundation of what is keeping us trapped in paradigms of internal and external war zones.

Our songs, languages, traditions, foods, rituals, and prayers—these are neither good nor bad. Force, by exclusion or by demanded inclusion, is the only roadblock to spirituality. All spiritual pathways are valid, except the ones that crush my soul or impede your connection to yours. Your highest self will help you ascertain the difference.

15
deep healing

Force. I don't know about you, but personally I am done being forced to fit into hierarchical structures. I have learned that the guard keeping me trapped therein was my shadow. Have you met yours yet? Your shadow is where your trauma lives. It is also the part of you that is in a constant state of growth.

As a society, we aren't terribly comfortable reckoning with this part, because we are operating from a survivalist mindset. Surviving doesn't leave much time for questioning our feelings and deeper motivations. To survive, my time must be spent being good, being moral, being normal, being smart, being fast, being strong, being productive, being attractive, being thin.

Stopping to question *why* I am trying to survive within this paradigm of attachments begets my favorite question: *Said who*?

When my awakening hit, I realized I simply couldn't keep going as I was; I had to stop and address my existential angst. Allowing my shadow to enter the conversation helped bring to the surface the parts of me that were attached to the expectations and judgments of the pain-triarchy. I also learned that my shadow wasn't *bad* or *good*, it was just the part of me that remains "under construction," for lack of better language. Each time I am able to answer another *"said who,"* a piece of my shadow becomes infused with light. This is what healing is.

The process is ongoing, hence, *evolution*. I will *always* be made up of my shadow and my light. It is only when I am familiar with both that I am able to function within the Golden Rule. For me, it was easier to see *all* of you before I could see *all* of me. In learning how to witness both *your* shadow and *your* light with empathy and respect, I was finally able to offer the same to myself. Within this context, caring is not just about comfort, nor is it just about kindness. True care, for self and others, is a process of holistic healing. Holistic, as in deep and all-encompassing. So grab your scuba gear.

Lemme explain by sharing a bit more about my healing journey. Prior to my awakening, I had no relationship with my shadow. I was just doing my best to *survive* within the family and the society into which I had been born. I didn't understand any of my motivations, regardless of whether I was doing something helpful or hurtful. What I lacked was any context for *why* we treat ourselves and each other as we do.

My introduction to my shadow began with a simple question. *Why do I feel like shit?* On paper I looked like I had it all, but in my gut I felt like I was nothing.

And so I began peeling back the many layers of hurt that had accumulated throughout our lifetimes. This hurt manifested in my current situation as follows. I felt hurt by my mother, by my family, by my friends, by the world, and by myself. I also thought the problem was ME. I was just taking it all too hard; I was just too *sensitive*. As a result, I had spent most of my life trying to *toughen up*.

At my lowest point, the universe stepped in and swept me up into the spiritual storm I mentioned. I could have turned things off at this point, and closed my eyes to what I was being shown. But I was curious. Could what I was learning at my Me University make me feel better?

Turns out it could, but I would have to put in the work. The knowledge I gained showed me that to heal, I would need to open the door to my soul and experience both my wonder *and* my wounds in equal measure. I had a tendency to not give either much time. In my wonder I could find faults, and in my wounds I would try to avoid the pain. I now take the time to intentionally sit with and explore all of my emotions and reactions.

Through this process, I learned to see my own light. I learned that I didn't need to *prove my worth* in exchange for love; I was lovable just for being me. I learned to see my power and claim it, as I did when I wrote those letters to my mother and my family.

I learned there is no right or wrong way to heal. Also, I learned that I can only heal what is mine. You too. Evolution, when we allow it, will take each of us where we are ready to go next. By choosing to keep learning, by choosing my family to be my partners in my growth, I also chose my team for my deep healing journey. "Team": once again it was the operative word. The serendipity is notable.

Team Food Chain provided a surprising vehicle to help me reconcile my attachment to victory and break through the core of my generational trauma with my kids. My *chains*, if you like. Deep cleansing breath.

To put things in perspective, Team Food Chain was part of our family from 2009 to 2018, spanning much of my kids' tweens and young adulthood, and my middle age. It wasn't just a project, it became our family business and it affected us all. Samantha was invited in, but opted to play a supporting role along with my mother and Craig. I've shared the story from my perspective; it was only recently that I heard Chad's and Samantha's. The difference in our perspectives has been both humbling and critical to our growth.

I'm glad we were able to make shit happen, but *how* it happened was symptomatic of an issue as important as hunger relief: starvation of the soul. By this I mean all three of us were desperately hungry for approval, belonging, and purpose.

I'll start with Chad. Here I thought I had been the wind beneath his wings, supporting the destiny of his golden future. Turns out he was trying to be the wind beneath mine. I wanted to go big or go home, and he wanted to help me experience that. Meanwhile, he was just a kid and couldn't tell me he was in over his head once things escalated from a big local initiative to a state-wide level. Internally, he was crumbling under the pressure to become a pillar of society.

I wish he'd had more space to just be a kid, and I wish I'd had more space to explore my talents in my own right. But we didn't. We were both in the clutches of our egos, our obligation to one another, his youth, my age, his queerness, my station in life, of wanting to belong, of perfectionism, of the need to achieve, and of our passion for justice work.

We were completely codependent with the pain-triarchy, *chained* to one another by an unconditional love that did not know healthy boundaries. A love that was vested in idealism. Only once I'd met my shadow, was I able to see the ways the pain-triarchy was in me and the ways that I had paid it forward.

I told Chad that in order to heal, he would have to create space to be mad at me. I gave him permission to go back to his childhood, remember what really happened, and how it made him feel. The idealism of pain-triarchy was the culprit for his despair, but I could see how I had been its accomplice. Chad's loyalty to me was prohibiting him from acknowledging this. I knew this, because it had been the same between Roberta and me.

As for Samantha, Team Food Chain had felt like an abandonment. Chad and I were out there "saving the world" and she was just trying to make it through a fucking day. It wasn't that she wasn't capable of joining us. It wasn't that she didn't share our concerns and desire for world repair. It was that her brain simply didn't function within the same perfectionist mindset. In a sense, her ADHD saved her from the clutches of idealism. On the other hand, it made her feel like shit, like she was a bad person, like she was selfish, and like she was playing second fiddle to Chad. She resigned herself to be the best supporting cast member possible, driven by her unconditional love for her brother and me.

Like Chad, I gave her permission to go back to her childhood and be mad at me too. She needed to see things through the lens of her ADHD. All the times I thought her spinning was just "girl stuff" I could relate to. I understood girl, right? As for the supporting role, it was one that misogyny had found me playing my whole life. But now I could see how I had been its accomplice.

Our family therapist played a critical role in our healing. We each went individually, but intentionally opened the door for him to cross reference as needed between us. By being brave enough to boldly dissect what really happened, we have been able to see that how things played out was vested in each of our survivalist tendencies. It may have appeared that we were thriving, but apparently that was not the case for any of us.

It wasn't until Chad and Samantha were able to share their side of things *without fear of hurting me* that our work truly paid off. An almost-win for hunger relief eventually became a win for the hunger within our souls. To fully be, to fully collaborate, to fully support each other, we would need to fully embrace the concept of failing as we succeeded *without fear*.

Was it great to hear that my passion for Chad's victories had also caused him pain? Was it great to hear that Samantha didn't feel like the main character in the story of her own life? No, of course not. But what I learned was a critical lesson, one that I am now in a position to pay forward. Acknowledging our pain did not negate our passion, it just enhanced the complexity of our growth.

Being authentic is an act of bravery that bridges the intersection of our shadow and our light.

In the writing of this book and the deep healing it took to get here, I am breaking through some significant generational trauma, not only between my kids and me, but also between my mother and me. Certainly we were effected by xenophobia, but at the core of our trauma was gender identity, which included internalized misogyny and homophobia.

Once I gave my kids permission to see all of me, it gave them a clearer picture of how deeply this trauma was embedded in my upbringing. It helped explain my actions and reactions, and in doing so explained theirs. I was able to give myself the same permission going back to my mother, albeit after her death. By enabling each of us to be witnessed in *full* transparency, we created the pathway necessary to heal the trauma and begin the process of becoming our authentic selves

Today Samantha, Chad, and I are focused on transitioning from survival to thrival behaviors and mindsets. We belong to each other, *as we are*, and we have committed to allowing each other to grow and evolve. Now when we trip, which we do, we have the tools and the language to recalibrate. We have worked hard to share our realities, to avoid expectations and judgments, and to maintain boundaries that are healthy and protective without being walls.

I share this interaction to highlight what it will look like to heal together as Generation WE. Accountability honors the entire story, not just the parts that fit a narrative that paints us above reproach. WE can't heal without acknowledging the whole truth about how it has been for both YOU and ME. WE have much to learn and to unlearn about our world, our country, our religions, our genders, our bodies, our emotions, and our abilities.

Deep healing can be really painful. Again, there is no right or wrong way, only the way that is right for your well-being. It is also complicated and highly personal. Circling back to the video game of evolution, each of our souls are on their own course of growth, even when we appear to be sharing the same experiences. What makes each of us unique is our response to the collection of experiences that WE have been gifted.

Therefore, each of us is responsible for our own healing. My mother was responsible for hers, me for mine, my kids for theirs. We may want to heal for each other, but we can't. None of us can take this on for anybody else. This only impedes the process for everyone.

Repeat, because this is really important: in regard to healing in general, you can only be responsible for yourself. What WE can do to stop the pain cycle is offer each other the intention to heal, the space to heal, the platform to heal, the empathy to heal, and the permission to heal.

Brushing things off as *I'm fine, everything's is good, I don't want to make waves*—this doesn't heal your pain, it is just a way of avoiding it. The same is true in reverse. Telling someone their pain isn't real, or worthy, or necessary doesn't heal their pain, it just adds to it.

For me, deep healing has required an enormous amount of conversation over a substantial period of time. I'm a bit like Socrates: I like to verbally hash things out. That's my method. These conversations have occurred predominantly with Samantha, Chad, our family therapist, and my healer.

My kids and I have always spoken frequently; now it is with intention. We take time out of our days to actively reflect on how we see things. We bounce our new perspectives and knowledge off of each other all the time. And we talk and we talk, and the patterns of the pain-triarchy begin to unravel. Within this, we are creating *better*: in our relationships, in the way we approach others, in the way we approach work, and in the way we approach LIFE.

Talking is just one way of tuning into the emotional intelligence required for deep healing. For you it might be music, art, reading, writing, therapy, or a combination of things. It doesn't matter. What does matter is finding ways to communicate with your shadow parts, again and again.

Because every time I thought I was done, another layer of conditioning would appear. I wanted to find something or someone to blame for this. Surely something *out there* was responsible for me feeling like shit and for the shitty things humans do to each other. But the more I healed, the more my capacity to witness the entirety of a given situation expanded.

Ouch. What I saw, again and again, was that I was as much a part of the problem as I was my own solution. It's hard to say what hurts more: what others did to me, what I did to me, or what I did to others. Yes, I was wronged, but I had also caused pain. I couldn't change what was, and neither could anyone else. All I could do was celebrate what I had learned and desire to do things differently going forwards.

A phrase I heard along the way resonated with me: "forgiveness is letting go of all hope for a different past."

I can't remember how it crossed my path, but it's true. Letting go of the past, that I could do. But what I couldn't do was forgive anybody else for what happened in my past or my present. It wasn't my place. The only person I could forgive was me: for any hurtful attachments, expectations, and judgments I had upheld. *The only person I could change was me.*

16
energy

As I fumbled my way to becoming ME, I began to notice the relationship between *energy* and me. If I'm talking about energy, you know Albert Einstein is going to come up. For an accountability reality check, the man was very misogynistic. He was also a brilliant student of life and offered many great quotes acknowledging his wonder of the universe. The one that resonates the most with me is, "Everything is energy and that's all there is to it."

If *everything is energy*, it occurred to me that the entire scope of my being was informed by a chain reaction of cause and effect, centered around the power dynamic within me, and between me and others. It is important to remind ourselves that the most prominent relationship in our lives is our relationship with self.

That said, when I put my relationship with myself, my mother, and my kids under a microscopic view, I discovered that the energy I witnessed could be broken down into three categories: toxic, limited, and infinite. I realized that how I interacted with myself and others created a ripple effect of connection that was defined by the energy exchange.

By ripple effect, I mean that when *everything is energy*, then everything gets paid forward. Energy is like water. It can be added to. It can evaporate and take another form. It can change its direction. But all in all, it is. And how we interact with it impacts both the present *and* the future.

I know this is getting kind of far out. Bear with me. The energetic ripple effect determines whether or not we are creating more of the same ... or whether WE are creating better. As I looked closer, I noticed that the same principles that applied to me and my family could be applied to ALL relationships.

Toxic energy in a relationship looks and feels like a cage in which you are held hostage by systems and beliefs that do not honor or respect your being. This includes how you treat yourself. Fear induces a double bind, making you feel like you have no autonomy in what you do or how you do it. Toxic energy places us in survival mode.

Limited energy looks and feels like a detente. Some trust has been established and a means for coexisting is possible, even within yourself. But only within a narrow framework. Fear is sidelined by *avoiding* issues that trigger it. The same is true for vulnerability. In this scenario, what you do and how you do it is your business, as long as it exists within the confines of the status quo. At its worst, limited energy results in complacency. At its best, it holds space for us to practice shifting from surviving into thriving.

Infinite energy, meanwhile, looks and feels like *freedom*. Your being is fully supported by trusted systems and beliefs. This enables you to be vulnerable and express your authentic self. What you do and how you do it is not limited by the pain-triarchy and its imposed status quo. You are free to succeed *and* fail in equal measure, because no parameters are placed on your growth potential. Thriving is an expression of infinite energy.

As I mentioned, generational trauma colors all of our interactions. Thus, when reading this, consider equally your relationship with yourself, your personal relationships, your professional relationships, and your relationship to the powers that be: government, religious affiliations, academic institutions, and the media, to name a few.

How do these relationships make you feel? Do you feel supported by them or judged? Is it safe for you to bring your authentic self into the relationship? Or does you being YOU trigger fear?

What we are witnessing in both the individual and collective landscapes of our lives is a massive shift in energy as WE redefine the power dynamics of the pain-triarchy. As WE orient away from the pursuit of victory, and towards success. Towards *better*. As WE evolve, so does our energy; we move from a toxic, limited exchange of energy, to a place of infinite flow. This is when better becomes possible.

Now, energy is also fluid, and so these categories are not fixed. Yes, the desired state is infinite energy, but it is unrealistic to think that all of our relationships will exist here. We are each of us works in progress. But as you shift, as you evolve, the energy between you and others will shift too.

Whenever my energy was in a toxic state, fear loomed like Pac Man, leaving little room for vulnerability and trust.

I got hung up on all the *shoulds* imposed by the pain-triarchy and its binary rules, confines, and hypocrisies. My safety felt threatened and I agreed with whatever was required of me as long as I felt like I belonged: to my mother, to my family, to my friends, my job, my faith, society ...

Whenever my energy was in a limited state, I functioned in what felt like a Venn diagram. In this energy state I was comfortable, because nothing was challenged. I was able to es-tablish a slice of trust within myself and with others through a shared understanding of the status quo and its require-ments. I was not, however, able to engage my vulnerability, and I avoided facing my fears. Within this structure, things hummed easily along, because the values and goals between me and others aligned, or at least appeared to align.

Whenever my energy was in an infinite state, it felt like an infinity circle was coursing through my body. I felt nurtured and nourished. When I was collaborating in flow with my cre-ativity, I felt energized. Whether I was healing or experienc-ing failure, I felt a deep sense of *knowing* that I was going to be ok, even when I was brought face-to-face with my fears.

Prior to my deep healing, I did experience infinite energy, just not very frequently. I would say infinite energy occurred at the times in my life when I was either unaware of the pain-tri-archy or when I intentionally pushed against it. I was able to first identify feeling infinite energy as part of my awakening. As both my wonder and my wounds began to present more clearly, I found myself wanting to experience them more fully.

Because I wanted to *feel better*, I learned how to *feel, better*, by engaging my sixth sense. I learned how to open the gateway to my highest self. Doing so enables me to make my unconscious conscious and to face my fears. This does not mean I am never afraid; it means that fear no longer keeps me in a state of toxic or limited energy.

I'm in a far different space from where I started. I can see now that I spent most of my life existing in limited energy, with toxic energy always taking me by surprise. On any given day my comfort in limited energy could slip into toxic energy without me even noticing the shift. I'd think I was on the same page, on what felt like equal footing, then a fear, be it mine or someone else's, would be triggered.

The energy would change abruptly. I'd find myself either the recipient or transmitter of fear, whether it was expressed as anger, manipulation, sulking, or other survival tactics. I came to realize my energy shifted frequently between these two states, because both toxic and limited energy are the by-products of the fear that is required to uphold the oppressive structure of the pain-triarchy.

I contend that as a collective, most of us are functioning between toxic and limited energy. We see this in our personal lives, in our professional endeavors, in our attempts to sustain the crumbling systems that govern us, in the aggressive reporting of the news, and the violent making of that news. Many of our concerns remain focused on maintaining hierarchies, as opposed to collaborating to create more possibilities.

Many of us claim to want change. But do we? Seems like how we would like that change delivered is pretty limited. "Change" would be great as long as ... a) it doesn't lessen our chances of victory or ... b) it directly benefits us.

The cornerstone of Generation WE is our ability to shift as a collective into infinite energy. This is what will be required to heal our generational trauma and start creating better.

Enlightenment is infinite energy. It exists in the space *between* polarities. We find enlightenment in the space *between* our analytical and intuitive selves, *between* our hearts and minds, *between* good and bad, *between* light and dark. Enlightenment is the quest for wisdom engaged by enacting empathy, compassion, curiosity, and wonder.

This gets a bit illusive, so lemme give you a visual. Think of energy in terms of a color wheel. Different shades and hues express your thoughts and feelings at any given moment of time. Yes, like the colors of the rainbow, which mirrors the chakra system.

When we are in toxic energy, we are only able to activate black and white. We can only see things in the binary. When we are in limited energy, we have access to the primary colors. Because we have taken a step out of the binary, a few more options exist. When we are in infinite energy, binaries do not exist. Function and flow occur simultaneously. The entire color wheel is activated and the possibility for color combinations is infinite.

When we engage infinite energy, we are creating from a place of freedom, a place where our success includes our failures. Each interaction becomes collaborative. If one thing doesn't work, we simply regroup and try another. If we outgrow something, we either throw it out or re-envision it. The trick of infinite energy is to keep fear outside of the relationship and address issues (even scary ones) by activating our intuition, critical thinking, and emotional intelligence.

Think of it this way—fear makes us scared, but wisdom makes us sacred.

17
time

With my new understanding of energy, life feels like a magic eye book. A phrase that popped into my head that says it all:

The seed to my potential lives in my perspective.

When I soften my vision, I can see the picture within the picture. I can see what I couldn't see before. Looking at humanity as a whole, yes, we are alive — but are we really living?

What I see in the "picture within the picture" is us scrambling to meet the expectations and avoid the judgments of the pain-triarchy. On the surface we look like we are functioning at a high level of productivity, but in reality we are being crushed by the myth that time is a scarcity. We are spread too thin. Just getting through the day is exhausting. The pressure to achieve has run amok and the culture of excess is creating lack, not more.

The mantra, *live each day as if it was your last*, is killing us, not fulfilling us. Body-mind-spirit. Who has time to eat, let alone breathe, contemplate, or be wise?

And then time stopped.

The pandemic whiplashed me, like many, into a suspended Neverland state. Watching it all unfold was both terrify-ing and unifying. While I will never be able to wrap my head around the devastation, personally I was relieved to get off the human hamster wheel of modernity.

What I learned during this global moment of pause is this:

To be human is to be alive: to survive. To be humane is to give a shit about how you live and the impact of your choices and your beliefs on others, and yourself: to thrive.

When WE look at our lives I want the "picture within the picture" to be a place of expansion, not desperation and exhaustion. For us to create this new imagery WE need to sof-ten ourselves and shift the lens of our perspective. WE need to unlearn the binary limitations and reactions of the pain-tri-archy and embrace our emotional intelligence instead. WE need to become interactive parents to ourselves and others. WE need to go deep into our generational trauma and heal it. There is no other way.

Therefore, now would be a good time to assess your ex-pectations and judgments. Trust me, you are carrying more than you think! You will have to identify what went well for you, what didn't. You will have to question what served you at one time, but no longer does. You will have to explore your belief systems by listening to other points of view without fear of buckling under their convictions. Simply put, you will have to be brave enough to find your authentic voice. Not only can you, only you can.

Remember, *everything is energy* and each energetic shift is part of a chain reaction. Just like our pain has been paid for-ward, person to person, so can our enlightenment be. One break in the pain cycle is one less cycle of pain that gets paid forward. One interaction that shifts to infinite energy paves the path for another's evolution.

I am just beginning this journey myself. It is a winding road, and I am on it with you. There is so much of our individual and collective unconscious that is still to be revealed. One thing that is clear: being humane takes time, so put away your stopwatch.

I don't have a road map to enlightenment, nor can I tell you what your personal infinite energy palette looks like. The process of evolving consciousness doesn't work that way. I can't tell you what *creating better* means to you, because *better* is highly personal. What I can tell you is that WE will only be able to create a better tomorrow when we focus on healing today.

And we must. The future is counting on us.

acknowledgements

The past seven years have been an intensely immersive experience in self-discovery and conscious evolution. Thanks to everyone who listened to me, questioned me, and healed with me. I would especially like to thank the following folks for helping me find my purpose, my voice, and most importantly, myself.

Ruby Warrington, working with you is like taking a master class in journalism with one of the wisest people I have ever met. Book doula, mentor, friend, and kindred spirit - out of chaos you located my story. Thanks for taking me under your wing, coaching me, and helping me get my vision out into the world.

Amy Lynn, our connection is core and my appreciation for you is enormous.

Linda Schuster, you believed in me from the get-go. Thanks for the friendship, guidance, and business acumen.

Bailey, Chasson, Danni, Grant, Kim, Kelsey, Leo, Molly, PJ, and

Robin - thanks for being gentle with my heart and encouraging my work.

Craig, your unyielding support means everything.

Chad and Samantha, to infinity and beyond always.

And last, but certainly not least, Roberta. You often said the gift of love was mine to share, thanks for helping me share it. I know from the beyond you're with me, rooting for the future.

about the author

Artist, author, and energist Abby Kamen is dedicated to reversing the tide of generational trauma with conversations about self-discovery and conscious evolution. In addition to her own projects, Abby collaborates with individuals and organizations vested in protecting our human rights and providing resources for our mental health and emotional well-being. She lives in Louisville, KY. Feel, better at www.abbykamen.com

www.ingramcontent.com/pod-product-compliance
Lightning Source LLC
Chambersburg PA
CBHW020252130626
46549CB00005B/2181